James Stokes Lectureship on Politics
New York University · Stokes Foundation

||||||||||||||||||||||||||||||||

THE ROLE OF POLITICS IN
SOCIAL CHANGE

Representative Government in the United States
by WILLIAM HOWARD TAFT, 1921

Sovereign States and Suits before Arbitral Tribunals and
Courts of Justice
by JAMES BROWN SCOTT, 1925

American Foreign Policies: An Examination and Evaluation
of Certain Traditional and Recent International Policies of
the United States
by JAMES WILFORD GARNER, 1928

The Pilgrim Fathers from a Dutch Point of View
by D. PLOOIJ, 1932

The Foundations of American Constitutionalism
by ANDREW C. McLAUGHLIN, 1932

Our Earliest Colonial Settlements: Their Diversities of Origin
and Later Characteristics
by CHARLES M. ANDREWS, 1933

The Puritan Pronaos: Studies in the Intellectual Life of New
England in the Seventeenth Century
by SAMUEL ELIOT MORISON, 1936

THE ROLE OF POLITICS
IN SOCIAL CHANGE

by

CHARLES EDWARD MERRIAM

NEW YORK UNIVERSITY PRESS

WASHINGTON SQUARE, NEW YORK

London: HUMPHREY MILFORD · OXFORD UNIVERSITY PRESS

1936

PREFACE

THE *following lectures were given at New York University in November 1935 in the series presented by the Stokes Foundation. The observations here outlined are based in part upon the writer's general experience and reflection upon government, but more particularly upon his recent membership of and relations with President Hoover's Research Committee on Recent Social Trends, President Roosevelt's National Resources Board, and the Social Science Research Council's Commission of Inquiry on Public Service Personnel. It should perhaps be said further that these lectures are a development of special phases of my work on* POLITICAL POWER *and of other forthcoming studies dealing more specifically and constructively with the emerging political philosophies and programs of our day.*

I wish to express here my appreciation of the services of my daughter Elizabeth in the preparation of this manuscript.

CHARLES E. MERRIAM

TABLE OF CONTENTS

		PAGE
Preface		VII
I.	Boycotting Government	13
II.	Putting Politics in Its Place	35
III.	The Philosophy of Pessimism and the Practice of Violence	61
IV.	Conservation and Change in Politics	79
V.	Strategic Controls	103
VI.	The Nature of National Planning	123
Index		145

THE ROLE OF POLITICS IN
SOCIAL CHANGE

I
BOYCOTTING GOVERNMENT

THE MODERN WORLD suffers from a lack of balance between what is called the political and what is called the economic; a lack of working interrelationship between these two, and between politics and economics and the larger social whole. This misunderstanding, obstructing the way to clear thinking and intelligent social action, is the result of a century of tragic misinterpretation of these relations, now producing its full effect in a period of sweeping change when adjustment is more than ever necessary.

Failure to deal effectively with social maladjustments and the distress they bring to vast numbers of the human race is full of the very gravest threats for the continuation of our civilization. In the moment of the greatest triumphs of the human mind over the forces of nature, we face the grim reality of violent social dislocation, of civil and international wars, of Vesuvian eruptions so full of hatred, violence, unreason, and impatience as to threaten the stability not merely of social or political order, but of our civilization and of the happiness of mankind.

The paragraphs immediately following are designed to illuminate some of the dark spots of our discontent, indicating later some possibilities of escape from the threat of impending collapse.

I approach this problem by examining

I. A set of influential theories distorting the role of the political by diminishing and decrying government—boycotting government we may fairly say—regarding it as a necessary evil, the work of the devil

II. A set of theories exalting the power and purpose of the state, and distorting its position in the social domain

III. The actual role of the government in social affairs not from the point of view of this particular moment of struggle but from that of broader observation and analysis

One of these mistaken interpretations of the "political" was that of anarchism, directed at the complete destruction of the state. Another was that of Marx and a group of collectivists who evolved a theory of anti-statism curiously combined with a practical gospel of pan-governmentalism. Another was the doctrine of the laissez-faire philosophers who narrowed down the functions of the state to the lowest possible terms, and extended a general challenge to the political. Out of these movements taken together there emerged what may fairly be characterized as the "boycott" of government. This doctrine of distrust of political action alternating with pangovernmentalism lies at the root of our present problem of social balance and security.

All of these theories were based upon a misconception of the nature and functions of political and social control, and all of them tend to confuse the social thinking of our own day.

The anarchist assumed that all forms of political control per se are undesirable, and that the good of society would be best promoted by abolishing them altogether. In place of the political principle there was substituted some cohesive element such as Proudhon's "justice" or Tolstoi's interpretation of the Sermon on the Mount, or Kropotkin's factor of "mutual aid." All of these systems identified political control with violence and the institutionalization of violence, and assumed that without this the state would no longer exist.

Many and indeed most of the anarchists—although not

all—were alienated from the state not only by the identifica-
tion of political association with violence, but by a false view
of the state as essentially the tool of an organization known
as capitalism. Many anarchists were indeed more concerned
with the modification of the economic system than with the
abolition of the use of force in social relations, as is evident in
the terroristic actions of one wing of the revolutionary anarchists. In a force institution anarchists saw a means of preser-
vation of the existing economic order, and reacted even more
violently, if this is an appropriate word in this connection,
against the purposes for which the state was used than against
the organization itself. They did not hate the state as much
as they did the social uses of the state. But in any event
anarchists did not analyze the nature of political control beyond the stage of characterizing it as a method of violence,
always in the service of oppressors.

Toward the end of the century the anarchist philosophy
tended to fade out of the center of the picture, yielding to the
more sharply defined outlines of individualism. In the broader
sense of course the anarchistic protest against the abuse of
violence is a continuing phenomenon, recurring from period
to period in the life of the race, rising from one neo-anarchism
to another in successive eras of brutalization of authority.[1]

The boycott of the state was far more effectively developed
by the protagonists of economic individualism and collectivism, respectively. This new interpretation of the nature of
social control was most fully and forcefully presented by the
classical economists on the one hand and Karl Marx on the
other, with clouds of adherents on either side.

These ancient prophets upset the modern world by their

[1] See C. E. Merriam, *Political Power* (New York: McGraw-Hill Book Company,
Inc., 1934), chapter V, "The Shame of Power."

one-sided assumptions regarding the nature of social organization, and the relative position of the economic and the political in human affairs. Standing midway between the older era of landed economy and a dawning era of industrialism, they were alike confused by the new trends developing around them, and were consequently led to unsound and disastrous conclusions regarding political and social organization.

Both were deeply impressed with the importance of a neglected economic factor in human relations, and the relative insignificance of other elements in the social process. Both were unimpressed with the significance of the state and of the political. Both were primarily concerned with the analysis of so-called "economic" operations and relatively indifferent to political institutions. They both tended to identify "economics" with social welfare, to the exclusion of politics, while at the same time they neglected important aspects of economics, such as consumption. They united in setting up the new economic theology.

The political theory of Karl Marx was a wilderness of confusion. It bore the unmistakable marks of the influence of the anarchistic philosophy and paradoxically of individualistic economics itself. The Marxian philosophy was not statist but anarchistic, explicitly and emphatically. Whatever may happen in the meantime, said Marx, ultimately "there will no longer be political power, properly speaking, since political power is simply the official form of the antagonism in civil society." The state will disappear when the class struggle comes to a close. The state is thus condemned and executed by definition, so to speak. Of course, if the political power is "simply the official form of the antagonism in civil society," and if that antagonism disappears, then by definition political power goes with it into oblivion. Then, theoretically, the coming society will be a stateless society, an anar-chistic grouping, without form and void, politically.[2]

What would take the place of the political order within society? To this Marx returned no answer, although the political steps in the assumption of authority by the prole-tariat were discussed on various occasions by him, but only as stages in the direction of the final emancipation from political organization.

Nor has the Marxian theory of the state been materially changed by the soviet leaders of our day. "The annihilation of state power," said Lenin, is the aim all socialists have in view. The apparatus of officialism must be overthrown. The substitution of the "massed power of the workers," or the dominance of "social habit" or some weird form of "auto-matic administration" are hinted at from time to time, but no essential modification is made of Marx's original and apostolic assertion that political power and the state are headed for the grave. In the transition period, political organ-ization and the use of violence are in full swing, but theo-retically these must be regarded as a preliminary stage leading up to the final day when political authority reaches the end of the road.[3]

Here is a blind spot, marking inability to see the political phase of human social relations. This may be attributed partly to the influence of contemporary anarchism, and partly to the predominance of classical economic assump-tions, not too closely scrutinized by those who took them over.

The Marxian absorption in the economic aspects of human

[2] See S. H. Chang, *The Marxian Theory of the State* (Chester, Pa.: John Spencer, Inc., 1931), for analysis of Marx's doctrine and of later Marxian commentators.

[3] T. B. Brameld, *A Philosophic Approach to Communism* (Chicago: The University of Chicago Press, 1933). J. F. Hecker, *Russian Sociology* (New York: Columbia University Press, 1915). Sidney and Beatrice Webb, *Soviet Communism: A New Civilisation?* (London: Longmans, Green and Company, Ltd., 1935).

organization was not, of course, accidental but the central feature of his ideology. Viewed as an organization of propaganda for the promotion of his social objectives, the Marxian doctrines were vigorous and effective, and will always be studied with interest by students of human manipulation.[4] Viewed as a protest against the overemphasis on abstraction seen in what has been called the meta-politics of Hegel, the historical significance of the Marxian counter-ideology is evident. It is meta-economics against meta-politics. But viewed as a scientific analysis of the political process, the reasoning of Marx is incredibly defective.

In the bizarre mixture of truth and error which constitutes the "dialectical materialism" the economic assumptions may almost escape notice, so quietly are they slipped in.

"In the *social* production which men carry on they enter into definite relations that are indispensable and independent of their will; these relations of production correspond to a definite stage of development of their material powers of production. The sum total of these relations of production [social?] constitutes the *economic* structure of society—the *real* [why real?] foundation on which rise legal and political structures and to which correspond definite forms of social consciousness." It will be observed that Marx glided over from *social* production in one sentence to *economic structure* in the next, appearing thereby to identify social production (whatever may be contained in this ample phrase) with economic structure. This social-production-economic-structure, he alleged, constitutes the *real* foundation on which legal and political structures rise. A realist might well inquire, however, how it is that "social production" includes "eco-

---

[4] See the acute and devastating analysis of the Marxian propaganda by H. D. Lasswell, *World Politics and Personal Insecurity* (New York: McGraw-Hill Book Company, Inc., 1935), pp. 128 *et seq.*

nomics" but not government and law? This was not a demonstration but a form of sleight of hand. Elsewhere Marx speaks in different terms of a "prevailing mode of economic production and exchange" and a "social organization necessarily following from it."[5]

Still again he asserts, differently now, that "the social organization and the state issue perpetually from the *life process* of definite individuals, but from these individuals not as they appear in their own or another's imagination, but as they really are, as they materially produce—thus as they act under definite material limitations, premises and conditions independent of their will." One might well inquire, Is this also the origin of the Marxian theory, or is Marx alone the great Undetermined?

Or again Marx involves himself in the obvious contradiction involved in the statement that "The mode of production in material life determines the general character of *social*, political and spiritual processes of life."[6] But what is the difference then between the social process of life and the process of production?

The ideal, in the reasoning of Marx, "is nothing else than the material world reflected by the human mind, and translated into forms of thought." He evidently soothes himself by the thought that "reflections" are not "real." Or is there another order of "reality"? There are his historical "laws" of economic evolution, but are these laws "material" or only "reflections of a pattern," which is, of course, also material?[7]

[5] *Critique.*

[6] An excellent statement of opposing theories is given by Charles W. Morris in his *Six Theories of Mind* (Chicago: The University of Chicago Press, 1932).

[7] I am not unaware that some passages in Marx and Engels indicate a broader view of the interrelations of the economic and the political; but the influence of his philosophy has followed the course indicated above. Cf. Sidney Hook, *Towards the Understanding of Karl Marx* (New York: The John Day Company, 1933).

The propositions of Marx regarding monism, materialistic monism, and economic or environmental determinism have little to do with the development of the body of his analysis and speculation. He might have made the same economic analysis with dualism instead of monism, idealism as well as materialism, and voluntarism as well as determinism. His dogmatism gives to his work an appearance of scientific quality, effective for propaganda purposes, but technically irrelevant.

What is the secret of Marx's attack on the Hegelian dialectic of idealism? It is found in his belief that the philosophy of the famous German "seemed to transfigure and glorify the existing state of things." In its Marxian form dialectic involves "the recognition of the negation of that state—because it lets nothing impose upon it, and is in its essence critical and revolutionary." [8] He found it useful, therefore, to reverse the Hegelian logic and base his system on the assumptions of materialism, rather than of idealism.

The truth is that the philosophical assumptions of Marx upon which so-called "scientific socialism" rested have nothing to do with his penetrating analysis of the trends of economic evolution. The tragedies of English industrial life vividly portrayed in the reports of the different commissions upon which he drew so heavily and so appropriately, the trends toward larger scale enterprise, the comment on the contemporary capitalism which he so keenly observed, all these might equally well have been made by Adam Smith or John Stuart Mill—or by Hegel using the very dialectic which Marx rejected. Neither monism, materialism, nor determinism, to say nothing of anti-statism, was essential to an accurate description and analysis of the social and economic trends of his time.

[8] Preface to *Capital*, second edition.

The same may be said of his conclusions regarding the importance of the collective ownership of the means of production; for this might follow from dualism, idealism, or voluntarism with equal validity. Indeed all this had already been developed by many thinkers, whom he chose to characterize as utopians or idealists, in contrast with himself as the "scientist."

We are dealing here, however, primarily with the overemphasis on a vague "economics" in the thought of Marx, and its consequences in an understanding of the political process. In the assumption or conclusion that social processes are primarily and basically economic, without analysis of the content of "economic," Marx really took over the assumptions of the laissez-faire economists; and the combination of the two has prevented the adequate analysis of the nature of the social and political process.

Marx's doctrine of class and class struggle worked in the same direction and with the same effect; namely, to distract attention from the political problems of society. The proletariat and bourgeoisie are asserted to be the two great and only classes. The state is only the official recognition of their antagonism, to disappear when the class struggle ceases with the triumph of the proletariat. [9]

Aside from the absurd conclusion that political organization comes to a close with the adoption of any particular economic arrangements, the concept of class is unclear and untenable. What is a class, and what are the common marks of members of a class? And how do we know that there are no other patterns or "classes" equally or more important? A class is a class, it appears, because of its economic basis. But

[9] "The executive of the modern state is but a committee for managing the common affairs of the whole bourgeoisie." (Manifesto.)

what is the economic again? Is it social production, social process, the life process itself as sometimes appears?

It is clear that groupings may be made on the basis of money income, although there are other forms of income; or on the basis of property holdings, although there are many forms of property and skills which have no money value; or in terms of employment of personnel in production; and that civil and political rights may be made to rest on these differentials, as historically they have in many cases. But many other classifications may be and are made on other bases, as race, religion, neighborhood, nation.[10]

In the Marxian theory, however, a further step is taken, and all classes are reduced to two. The inconvenient middle class remains, inconvenient because it may contain worker and employer in the same person; and to cap the climax of this solemn series of assumptions, the whole set of political relations is relegated to the position of a temporary brawl between these two economic groups—to be ended by the victory of one and the end of government.

The shocking naïvete of these conclusions is obscured by the vigor and penetration of other parts of Marx's analysis, in which his intelligence is dissociated from the urgencies of a propaganda system, apparently important even in a fatalistic world. The only use of the state would be the forceful expulsion of the exploiters, and a temporary regime of violence, to be superseded, however, by the non-governmental, non-class organization of society. In any case the only value system recognized is that which may be characterized as "economic," but omitting other forms of social values and only vaguely defining or delimiting the "economic."

[10] On the conception of class see the *Encyclopedia of the Social Sciences*, articles "Class" by Paul Mombert (volume III, pp. 531-536) and "Caste" by A. L. Kroeber (volume III, pp. 254-256).

When he discusses coöperation in the labor world, Marx becomes far more appreciative of the nature of social organization. Thus he finds that "All combined labor on a large scale requires, more or less, a *directing authority*, which secures the harmonious working of the individual activities and performs the general functions that have their origins in the action of the combined organism, as distinguished from the action of its separate organs." But, in general, political organization and direction remain with him in the clouds of anarchism.

While Marx oscillated between acute analyses of capitalistic phenomena on the one hand and fulminations of revolutionary propaganda on the other, and thus distracted attention from the meaning of the political in human affairs, the doctrine of Ricardo taken as a representative of the classical economists was almost equally distracting and curiously enough arose from the same general point of view. It may seem preposterous to class together the great advocate of economic collectivism and the great advocate of economic individualism, but fundamentally they were alike in the interpretation of life in economic terms. If Marx was an economic determinist outright, Ricardo assumed the harmonious operation of economic forces as the *summum bonum* of human existence and believed that if these forces were allowed to operate with a minimum of interference the highest ends of man would best be served.

The classicists did not outlaw the state as did Marx, but elbowed it aside to the outer edge of human activity. Implicitly rather than explicitly, they contrasted the inherent excellence of the free "economic" system with the inherently dubious "political" mode of direction.

The philosophy of Marx and Mill leaned heavily to the

side of pleasure-pain interpretation of human behavior. In neither was there a large place for the vast areas of the human spirit in which sacrifice and devotion rule the hour and determine the lines of human direction. In the Marxian doctrine the individual was driven along by the compelling necessity of the economic *entourage*, which apparently had no room for sacrifice and surrender, in theory at least. Even the stormiest revolution was apparently an inexorable economic event, in which the urge to control the instruments of production was sufficient to animate the most sluggish and furnish him with a complete equipment of motivation.

In general the philosophy of both was developed as if the goods of life were in the main what we call producers' goods— and as if the great sweep of enthusiasm and devotion which plays so great a role in the lives of many men and women did not exist—or could be safely ignored in the calculations which determine our behavior.

This is not intended to disparage the great services rendered by classicists and Marxists in directing attention to the neglected importance of economic relations to political structure, function, process in their day. The Hegelian abstractions had gone so far as to draw attention aside from the ways of life among which the economic are of vast significance. To some extent, although not to so great a degree, the natural-law philosophy had tended in the same barren direction. Marx and Ricardo recalled philosophers to the consideration of important factors in politics early considered by the Greek thinkers, but receiving inadequate attention. In this sense they might have helped to enrich the content and meaning of the political, but unfortunately their influence was directed in the opposite course. Marx gave thumbs down to the state and Mill held down the bounds of state activity to the lowest possible terms. Unwittingly they both paved the way for a long period of overemphasis on the economic aspects of life, an exaggeration beyond all reason of one phase of human existence—a barrier to an adequate understanding of economic forces in relation to social forces, serving to relegate the political to the limbo of the necessary evil. They both recall Adam Smith who had already laid the foundations of their doctrine when he found that the rise of property occasions the establishment of government. The passions of men may be held in check without magistrates, he observes, but "avarice and ambition in the rich," "hatred of labor and love of present ease and enjoyment on the part of the poor" require some form of government. "Where there is no property, or at least none that exceeds the value of two or three days labor, civil government is not so necessary." [11]

Many members of the laissez-faire school were far more vigorous in their attacks upon state activity than Mill, and this liberal advocate is selected for the very purpose of showing how under the most favorable circumstances the role of political control was fundamentally limited by this school. The assumption was that the natural laws of economics if left uninterrupted by the rude hands of politics would work out the destiny of mankind most speedily and fully. Even the broad and genial Mill could not conceal his indifference to the creative role of the "political" in social relations.

While the doctrine of some classicists was far more temperate in statement than others, and while they did not avoid as did Marx the discussion of detailed problems of governmental organization, and while they did not predict the ultimate disappearance of the state, nevertheless their funda-

[11] Adam Smith, *The Wealth of Nations* (London: G. Routledge and Sons, 1890), Book V, Part II.

mental interest was much the same as that of Marx; namely, an obsession with the operation of economic forces. Just as the *deus ex machina* in Marx was an incredibly vague mass of undigested "economic" relations, so their god was evidently the natural harmony of a set of forces, called "economic," whose normal result would be the highest happiness of mankind. In general, leave these natural forces alone, said Ricardo, and they will evolve the greatest good of the greatest number. Leave these natural forces alone, said Marx, and they will evolve the classless society and the proletarian heaven.

Each dealt with an economic system, as if it had somehow come into being in a political vacuum, or could operate in such a vacuum—stateless and classless in one case; with a minimum of interference in the other. Each proceeded as if there were laws of production, modes of distribution, patterns of consumption—all arranged without regard to the intervention of any political agency, and even without regard to any cultural agency, it appears at times. Both ignored the social function of political direction, ignored or understated. They helped to set up the nineteenth-century plan of two worlds—one of which, politics, is vile; and the other of which, economics, is from on high.

The historical value of these doctrines as a protest against the current tendency to ignore important aspects of economic activity must be fully recognized, but likewise the disastrous effect of these doctrines when continued after the period of their greatest utility and when projected into other situations must be just as freely recognized. While the Marxian anarchists proceeded to build up a powerful state, the anti-governmental industrialists built up government in industry itself.

A far more direct attack upon state systems of control

was made by the sociologist, Herbert Spencer, in whose hands the natural "social order" became sacrosanct. The most fundamental law, he reasoned, is that of "conduct and consequence." Hence, how can any interference with this law on the part of government find a justification? The "sins of legislators" sums up in vivid language with telling illustrations the folly of attempting to advance through the agency of political controls and devices. [12] It remained difficult indeed to find any justification for government at all, if the Spencerian logic were carried ruthlessly to its ultimate conclusions. The anarchist Vaillant justified violence on the theory of Herbert Spencer.

But while Marx and Ricardo had invoked economic controls to take the place of any other, the Spencerian doctrine substituted not *economic* but social laws as the controlling factor in the determination of human behavior. Thus the sociological blessing was added to the economic eulogy of natural laws, and Smith, Marx, and Spencer—great names to conjure with—were all combined in the boycott of the state.

In the last generation the extreme forms of the laissez-faire theory on the one hand and the anarchist-socialist theory on the other have been modified by later theorists to some extent. [13] Mr. Hoover declared in his *Challenge to Liberty* that no apostles of the laissez-faire doctrine remained, with rare exceptions.

Nevertheless, with the rise of the movement toward social control of industry in Western Europe and America, there has come violent denunciation of the role of government in

[12] Herbert Spencer, *The Man v. The State* (New York: D. Appleton and Company, 1888).

[13] F. W. Coker, *Recent Political Thought* (New York: D. Appleton-Century Company, Inc., 1934). C. E. Merriam and H. E. Barnes, *Recent Political Theory* (New York: The Macmillan Company, 1924).

the process of social control. A former president of the United States Chamber of Commerce asserting that "the best government is the worst" expressed with unusual vividness the attitude of those who conduct what may fairly be termed a boycott of government in our own day—an attitude running back to the philosophies of Ricardo and Marx and based upon the same misunderstanding of the role of control systems in modern social organization.

Many others, less outspoken, have in practice acted upon a like theory of the relative unimportance of the state and of political action, challenging every extension or modification of governmental function, especially in the field of industrial relations, except aids in the form of bounties, subsidies, tariffs. For more than a century in which industrial conditions were being profoundly modified by science and technology, every move in the direction of governmental regulation has been challenged by a philosophy based upon the assumed danger of political action. Child labor, workman's compensation, social insurance, regulation of working and living conditions, blue-sky laws regulating types of securities—all have been obliged to run the gauntlet of critics of the state, basing their attacks upon the misunderstanding of the role of the political in social arrangements. "Less government in business," "no competition of public with private business," "no interference with business" were common slogans in the long controversy over the development of social control in newly developing social relations. In the organization of propaganda the most convenient devil was found in socialism or communism, but in reality the assault was directed against the readjusting role of the political in human association, except as the government might be required for purposes of internal or external protection.

Paradoxical as it may seem, throughout this struggle the Marxian philosophy likewise exalted the role of the "economic" in human affairs, preaching "economic determinism," "economic" class organization, the inevitable destruction of government as an ideal condition of human organization. In practice, to be sure, social democrats were favorable to the movement in behalf of social regulation of industrial forces, but theoretically many continued their barrage against the state and asserted their lack of faith in its possibilities. In the case of orthodox communists this was varied by unending attack upon the whole system of legal and political order developed in the nineteenth century, and by an exaltation of the role of violence as an instrument of social change, and of arbitrary dictatorship as its agent.

From the point of view of the student of political ideas, these anti-governmental doctrines may be classified as the reaction from opposite types of exaggerations. The glorification of the state reached its climax about the middle of the nineteenth century in the philosophical form developed by Hegel and the juristic form developed by John Austin. The court philosopher of Berlin presented *Der Staat* as the highest type of human association, the ultimate form of reconciliation of the individual will with that of the external will around him. The great German philosopher moralized the state; he surrounded it with all the adornments of philosophical elaboration; he gave it the blessing of one of the greatest philosophical minds of the time. Uninterested either in political reforms or in industrial situations, he saw in the state the supreme expression of moral integration and moral purpose. While few really read the obscure and difficult pages of the great philosopher, his ideas trickled through many channels into the thought of his time and exercised a far-reaching influence on theories and practices of government, especially on the continent of Europe.

At about the same time across the Channel, an almost equally difficult writer, John Austin, developed the doctrine of sovereignty to its highest form.[14] Like Hegel, this thinker was also indifferent to political reform and not concerned with industrial change, but solely as a jurist developed the doctrine of the legal omnipotence of the state.

In the elaborate Austinian theory the state is legally illimitable, legally despotic, legally irresistible. The state is not the antithesis of liberty but the necessary condition of liberty—the originator and protector of liberty. As Dicey the great British publicist stated the idea, somewhat later, the British Parliament is legally supreme. It cannot legally be resisted. If it orders that all blue-eyed babies be put to death— that is the law. Practically such commands may not be obeyed, but legally, in the narrower and stricter sense, they cannot lawfully be opposed.[15]

Neither the Hegelian theory nor that of Austin, sharply formulated and impressive as they were, had any immediate implications of governmental action. Neither was interested in the extension or modification of state activities in any special direction, in democracy, in socialism, in reformism of any description.

But building on the earlier, sixteenth-century doctrine of the great French publicist, Bodin, they constructed a theory of the state which gave it at once juristic omnipotence and moral sanction. The immediate influence of neither was large, although the Hegelian ideas had their effect on the dignity of

[14] John Austin, *Lectures on Jurisprudence* (London: J. Murray, 1832).
[15] See my discussion of Austinianism in *History of the Theory of Sovereignty since Rousseau* (New York: Columbia University Press, 1900).

German officialdom. This doctrine contained, however, no elements of a social or economic program, and indeed the Hegelian abstractions might be utilized in a policy of indifferentism toward the passing world. The Austinian theory, strongly as it emphasized the omnipotence of the sovereign, accompanied the laissez-faire economists' most influential hour, and was in no sense significant in its effect on contemporary social policy. The Austinians exalted the power of Parliament but did not amplify a program of parliamentary activity.

As has already been indicated, the Marxian theory advanced the doctrine of the futility of the state and predicted the ultimate extinction of all formal government. This was originally and remains to this day the official position of the professional Marxians. In practice, of course, the demand for the common ownership of the instruments of production inevitably emphasized the extension of the functions of the governmental agencies, although Marx was not a Hegelian or an Austinian.

The social democrats in Germany and elsewhere developed a platform and a program advocating the extension of the functions of the state both in the field of ameliorative social legislation and in the larger domain of socialization of industries. In its later communistic phases this movement, while theoretically advocating anarchism and repudiating democracy and parliamentary institutions, advocated the extensive employment of government in the form of a dictatorship with both the dignity of the Hegelian state and the legal irresistibility of the Austinian body politic.

In more recent times there has appeared the doctrine of the totalitarian state—a restatement of the political theory of Bodin, Austin, and Hegel, but with a far wider program directed toward the promotion of nationalistic aims, and organized in dictatorial form. One of the chief elements in the argument of the totalitarian state is, however, its hostility toward collectivism in the economic sense of the term. The totalitarian statists are willing to go any length in what is called nationalization, but not "socialization"—a distinction somewhat tenuous theoretically and practically fraught with large possibilities of state expansion in more than one direction. If we start with the conviction that anything may well be nationalized or anything may be militarized, it becomes easy to find that anything may be socialized, if, as, and when it is deemed necessary by those in possession of the instruments of authority.[16]

What is called totalitarianism is really the rediscovery of the doctrine of sovereignty, well established in the sixteenth century, by nations which have more recently come to national life and realization of it. But they have not yet learned the background of usage and custom which has grown up around this doctrine in the last three hundred years,[17] and start again *de novo*, as if nothing had been learned about the supremacy of the state. They might profitably have read Bodin's doctrine of sovereignty in the sixteenth century, or more appropriately in Germany have read the work of Meinecke on *Staatsräson*—the most brilliant exposition of the development of the idea of the majesty of the commonwealth.

These later doctrinaires have added nothing to the theory of the sovereignty of the state but have merely confused legal

[16] For statements of the totalitarian doctrine see F. W. Coker, *Recent Political Thought*, chapter XVII. Herman Finer, *Mussolini's Italy* (London: V. Gollancz, Ltd., 1935). H. W. Schneider, *Making the Fascist State* (London: Oxford University Press, 1928). On Nazi political theory see F. L. Schuman, *The Nazi Dictatorship* (New York: Alfred A. Knopf, 1935). E. Voegelin, *Der Autoritäre Staat* (Vienna: Verlag von Julius Springer, 1936).

[17] For doctrinal position of the totalitarians see chapter III.

omnipotence with a practical omnicompetence. They have alarmed those who are concerned over the question whether the holders of power understand its basic limitations, the finer shadings of the relation between the legal rulers in their plenitude of technical authority and the bulk of the community from whom habitual obedience must issue in a stream of assent on which all authority floats.[18]

For the moment, the totalitarians occupy the difficult position of opposing economic collectivism with aggressive nationalism. They insist upon the utter subordination of individual interest to the national or state interest, sweeping aside many of the buffer procedures which have been utilized for the purpose of minimizing the abuse of authority. They breathe out the fire of militarism, and at the same time make use of the fear of collectivism as a means of support. Insofar as collectivism is international in design this is a tenable position, but insofar as collectivism involves the subordination of the individual interest to that of the collectivity, the difficulty is far greater. Even if politics does not always follow logic, the swirl of social currents underneath these forms is equally full of difficulty and menace. At any moment nationalization, militarization, socialization, may run together, emerging in some new pattern of power and some new program of action.

The result of the clash between opposing doctrines, seen in Hegelianism, Austinianism, collectivism, totalitarianism on the one side and anarchism, laissez faire, anarchistic socialism, governmental boycottism on the other side, has been the setting up of artificially sharp lines of difference between the political and the economic. The tendency has been to relegate

[18] See C. E. Merriam, *The Making of Citizens* (Chicago: The University of Chicago Press, 1931), for a comparative study of civic cohesion in modern nations, and other volumes in the same series.

rational discussion to the limbo of emotional reactions and slogan-symbols, instead of detailed analysis of specific situations in their social setting and with full appreciation of the problem of social control. In this frame of mind, toleration is thrown to the winds. The determination of policies tends to become the function of those who hold the force that determines where authority rests at a given moment.

Of these different patterns it is difficult to say which has been the largest contributor to unbalancing the conception of the role of the political—whether the Hegelian moralizing of the state, or the Austinian's legal omnipotence, or the totalitarian omniactivity of the nation, or the laissez-faire doctrines of Mill and the classical economists, or the Marxian demand for the elimination of the state, or the collectivist doctrine of the omnicompetence of the community.

But it is clear that together they have produced in their interaction an atmosphere in which calm and rational consideration of the role of the governmental in social relations has become most difficult when most necessary—indeed, in many lands has ceased to exist. Rage tends to become more important than reason and concussion is more relied upon than discussion. If this were a remote battle of conflicting ideas alone, the world might await the decision with proper patience, but unfortunately the peace, security, comfort of millions of men are involved in a sprawling struggle the outcome of which none can safely predict.

II

PUTTING POLITICS
IN ITS PLACE

TO SEE CLEARLY what political control means in our times, it is necessary to take a broad view of the problem of social control; to look at the political alongside of other systems which together make up the network of human control and organization.

The analysis of this control process may be approached from very many different points of view. Thus it is possible to examine the motives which impel or induce allegiance and conformity to patterns of behavior. Divine right, the social contract, the pleasure and pain calculus of the Utilitarians, the desire formula (libido) of Freud and his disciples; any of these and others may be invoked in an attempt to provide an explanation of the rise and operation of control systems in social and political organization.

Or it is possible to look at controls in terms of mechanisms—to observe various institutional devices, such as legislative, executive, administrative, judicial, parties, pressure groups, and their rules and modes of activity.

Or it is possible to set up different groupings of interests, as religious, economic, cultural, political, and examine the various forms of pressures exerted by them in the control struggle.

In general, the first method has fallen short of success by reason of the lack of an adequate individual and social psychology; the second by overemphasis on the mechanisms

[35

apart from their functions.[1] The structures may be so far isolated from their uses that they take on an artificiality quite remote from the realities of life. Structures, forms, rules, and interpretations of them are useful but inadequate to the understanding of the political process. It is not enough to know, for example, that there is a legislative body with two chambers, one having one hundred and the other two hundred members. This so-called legislative body may be a mere form, as the old Roman Senate became, or a modern city council under a boss, or some legislative body under a military dictatorship. In these instances the control process has shifted from the formal agency to some informal agency otherwise organized and disposed.[2]

With alternating tensions and tempos the extent and intent of politics change, and of course the structural organization with them. These tensions and emergencies are of the essence of politics. To proceed otherwise is to navigate as if the ship would never meet a storm. Tensions in politics are not indeed emergencies but really normal in expectancy. The abnormal is normal, it might be said, with perhaps a little exaggeration. And the tragedies of politics often arise from the fact that the community morale painfully built up to support one situation becomes malaise in another and different case. Tradition, which is essentially a reduction of the voluntary to the automatic, and thus an efficient instrument in the social or political process, may by the same logic become an automatic obstruction to necessary change, and thus an automatic brake on advancement. The sacred animals may be-

---

[1] An adequate discussion of this broad field is obviously not to be expected here.

[2] On the broad subject of the relationship between structure and function see L. K. Frank, "Structure, Function, and Growth," in *Philosophy of Science*, II, 2 (April 1935), pp. 210-235; J. H. Woodger, *Biological Principles* (New York: Harcourt, Brace and Company, 1929).

come the shield of the enemy and lead to the defeat of the group they were presumably protecting.

The organizational aspects of the political may be over-emphasized to a point where they obscure rather than illuminate the actual trend of the real governmental process. This may proceed to such an extent that the tool of society or a given group becomes its master, and operates against its own basis. Thus centralization—a useful device in certain situations—stands in the way of local and personal development. Or decentralization instead of serving as a useful protection against central congestion may stand in the way of the life and growth of the community.

The same may be true of any governmental agency or instrument at various times. Either fear of the executive or desire for a vigorous executive; either distrust of legislatures or overconfidence in representation as a means of determining policy; either dislike of courts or obsession with the judicial process per se; any of these exaggerations may lead to mal-functioning of what was once an effective agency of the group. In what I have often called the "moving equilibrium" of politics, the relative values may remain the same for a long period of time, but they may also shift with great rapidity, as strategic points may shift in a battle, and the guns may fire now this way and now that. In war this is well understood, but in the arena of civil politics is less readily recognized. In war the objectives of the struggle are not confused with the principles of military warfare, but in politics the social objectives sometimes are confused with the techniques of government itself. Thus a device of society may stand in the way of the life of the society itself. The famous Frankfort Convention in 1848 deliberated over the bill of rights until the opposition rallied its forces and dissolved the convention. Communists were captured in Germany because they would not go over the grass which must be kept free of human feet.[3]

The intimate understanding of social controls is obscured by the different names attached to what may be much the same thing in another division of human activity. Thus a sharp but imaginary line is often drawn fixing the boundaries of political and economic control as if there were some inherent and absolute difference between them. It has already been shown how the conceptual background of this judgment has been laid in the powerful philosophical systems of Marx and Mill. But in reality the family, the church, the economic organization have traditionally been and still are important control systems alongside political.[4] The control devices of all of them run parallel to the political, or at times at cross purposes with the political.[5]

In all of them, basic patterns of association, with appropriate skills, instruments, processes, are developed historically and at present. The government of the family, the government of the church, the government of industry are highly developed, each in its domain, and intimately related to the governmental government, alternately threatening and appealing to their own control systems. Even among outlaws there is law, order, justice, discipline.[6]

In early times and even yet in many portions of the earth, the family control system was of prime importance, and much or most government was familial government. Sir Robert Filmer in his famous *Patriarcha* traced the origin of the divine right of kings back to the paternal beginnings of authority,

[3] See further discussion of this point in C. E. Merriam, *The Making of Citizens.*

[4] See C. E. Merriam, *Political Power*, chapter II, "The Family of Power."

[5] See C. E. Merriam, *Civic Education in the United States* (New York: Charles Scribner's Sons, 1934), chapter IV, "Concurrent Agencies of Civic Education."

[6] C. E. Merriam, *Political Power*, chapter III, "Law Among the Outlaws."

and on down to the seventeenth-century incumbents of England. With the transition from landed to industrial economy, with the abandonment of the hereditary transmission of political power, with the rise of the factory, the school, the hospital, the influence of the family upon political power patterns has diminished. None the less, its significance in social and political control is still of major rank. Small groups of families still wield enormous power as in Japan and in any case the foundations of social and political control may be laid in the familial training and in political precepts inculcated in family association. Many millions of families help to hammer out patterns of dominance, subordination, coöperation, which are of inestimable value to the state makers and operators. It is only when families or groups of them begin to sabotage the law that the influence of this small unit begins to be realized by the mightier, as when the Italians undertook to change the names of German families in the Tyrol, Weiss to Biancho, or Pferd to Cavallo.

The system of religious government and controls is likewise intimately related to the political, and indeed, as in the case of the family, identical from time to time. The head of the state may still be the head of the church. In the main, however, especially in the western nations, the principle of separation of church and state prevails, and the two control systems are to a considerable extent segregated. Yet the far-reaching influence of religious attitudes toward political power still continues. Law and morality interpenetrate in inextricable fashion, at many common points. Church and state no longer have their separate courts for their own subjects and their separate places of detention, but the church still prays for the state, and the state relaxes its power of taxation over the property of the church. As it becomes a moral duty to obey the law, so it becomes a legal obligation to protect the institutions and much of the moral code prescribed by the church.

The precise determination of the relative spheres of influence accorded to the value system outlined by the ecclesiastical authorities on the one side and the political on the other has been a subject of interminable speculation for centuries and still remains a contentious subject in western states. That the period of sharp and dramatic conflict is by no means ended is evident in the present-day struggles between Mussolini and the Holy Father, between Hitler and the churches of Germany, between the Soviet government and the churches of Russia. In these colorful contests may be seen anew the age-old struggle to determine the metes and bounds of the political and religious. The varying types of control are beautifully illustrated in the desperate efforts of the competing groups to sway the attitudes and behavior of the population to whom their appeal must be made.

In an intimate study of any of these contests is seen the nature and scope of the control systems available to each party to the conflict, and the strategy of the struggle as conditioned by the weapons available to each. To trace, for example, the struggles of Hitler successively with the Jews, the Catholics, and the Lutherans, and to observe the competition in symbolisms, ideologies, and force[7] is to obtain an admirable view of the inner secrets of the control system which operates through these diverse agencies. What, it may be asked, are the decisive factors which finally incline the multitude one way or another and pave the road to a definite decision?

[7] Paul Kosok, *Modern Germany* (Chicago: The University of Chicago Press, 1933), chapter on "Symbolism."

Bergson declares in his *Two Sources of Morality and Religion* that there are two factors in morality—one found in the nature of an imposition by authority and the other an inducement or persuasion. On the side of inducement or inspiration, obviously the political may compete with the moralistic for influence on the patterns of human conduct, through its heroes, memorials, and symbolisms of varying types; or in other instances there may be a concurrent action, each reënforcing the other.

Again, organizations centering around land, manufacturing, commerce, trade, finance, guilds, trading companies, corporations, cartels, trades unions, coöperatives have exercised many kinds of social control from time immemorial down to our day. From time to time they have clashed with or coöperated with the state, the church, the family, the social group, as interests, values, personalities, social tensions, inventions, discoveries came and went across the stage of existence.[8] At times they have dictated terms to the nominal holders of political authority, and at other times have abjectly submitted; on other occasions compromised and combined. At all times these groups have presupposed the existence of some legal order, some notions of justice, some set of moral values, some familial associations with which they must reckon in their calculations. For long periods land and political power went along together in a system of hereditary transmission of double authority. The landlord was the political lord as well in one and the same person. The establishment of the right of eminent domain transferred this power over land to the state, but this does not mean that the state actually undertook the management of all landed properties. Nor did the adoption of the principle of "business affected

[8] See C. E. Merriam, *Political Power*, chapter II, "The Family of Power."

with a public interest" involve the complete assumption of the regulation of all such enterprise in all its details.

At all times there have been borderline relations between political and industrial groups of a type so blended and combined as to make sharp differentiation between them impossible, as in our day the relations between the Bank of England and the government of England, or the relations between the United States government and the Federal Reserve Bank, or the London Passenger Transport Board, or the long series of quasi-governmental undertakings which are spread around the world. Broadly speaking, these arrangements are not exceptional or abnormal, but are the usual type that might be expected to appear in time of tension or at other periods when accommodation and adjustment are indicated by the balance of forces involved. It is inevitable that each special group should aspire to greater power and reach out to obtain it; but it is equally inevitable that none should obtain complete authority, except in some moment of extraordinary tension, such as a war, a famine, a plague, and not always then.

It is not surprising that in our day some theoreticians and indeed some practitioners should attempt to develop too exclusive lines of difference between what they may call "economic" and "political" activities, where the experienced observer of social trends and problems in various periods of social development is unable to discover any adequate ground for such exclusive differentiation. On the contrary he sees exaggeration and disproportion in the mistaken efforts to twist a temporary conflict of interest or ideas into a permanent principle of social process and organization—an exaggeration out of which incalculable confusion and disorder arise.

A closer examination of the controls of economics and politics reveals the truth that their differences are often too sharply accentuated, or are characteristic only of a single phase of political or economic evolution rather than of a continuing process. [9]

The two great forms of fluid "control" have been those of *gold* and *government*, using gold as a term for the pecuniary order in which money appears as a common denominator of many sets of values, and government as a term for community power expressed in the body politic. The wide range of human values reached with fluid power in the form of gold magnifies the sweep of the pecuniary order of things, and tends to induce the idea that gold is omnipotent and irresistible. But the limits of gold are always obvious to all but the cynic, for it cannot readily purchase the family, the church, or the nation. Prices are not quotable on the mother's sale of her baby, or the priest's sale of the cross, or the soldier's sale of his country. And it is also forgotten that the status of gold itself may be determined by government, using that as a name now for the political society. The coin is coin of the realm. Overnight conscription or the prison could turn all one's gold into naught. Inheritance itself is a creation of the law. Always there are human values peeping out that do not recognize the sovereignty of gold, and that behave in irregular ways.

From one point of view, government and gold may be viewed as contrasting methods of manipulating behavior, and we may compare the right to sign checks with the right to sign a military order. Which is stronger in a clash? Can gold buy the army or can the army take the gold? It is said that in the first Hitler Putsch of 1923 his soldiers could have taken the gold in the vaults of the Bank of Munich but were delayed by the insistence of the cashier on having two names signed to the receipt—until it was too late.

[9] *Op. cit.*, pp. 8-13, for discussion of the political.

Washington's soldiers at Newburgh offered to make him
king, it is said, if he would agree to give them their back pay
upon mounting the throne, in which case their steel would
have been transmuted into gold—or paper.

More than one war has been checked by bankers unwill-
ing to make the necessary loans, but more than one bank has
been taken over by conquering armies.

A statement of the problem in the form of a contrast between steel and gold is a dangerous oversimplification of a
question far more complex than this query would indicate.
Money is not a commodity apart from the political control of
the community and social values. Banking and credit institutions do not stand aloof from the group of which they are
part. Nor does steel—the political organization of the community—exist alone, exist apart from the social structure in
which it must function. Coin and credit demand the protection of the government. No army now lives wholly upon the
country but advances with the help of the exchequer and a vast
equipment of munitioning, provisioning, and transport. [10]

Current definitions and terminology do not aid greatly in
the clarification of this question. To say that politics is concerned chiefly with the state, and economics with wealth and
business, still presupposes an understanding of just what the
state includes and what business includes. [11] Mitchell declares
that economics "is a science of human behavior engaged in

[10] "I draw the conclusion," says Keynes, "that, assuming no important wars and
no important increase in population, the *economic problem* may be solved, or at least
within sight of solution, within a hundred years. This means that the economic
problem is not—if we look into the future—the permanent problem of the human
race."—*Essays in Persuasion* (London: Macmillan and Company, 1931), pp. 365-366.

[11] For definitions of politics see J. W. Garner, *Political Science and Government*
(New York: American Book Company, 1928), chapter I. For definitions of economics see Paul W. Homan, *Contemporary Economic Thought* (New York and
London: Harper and Brothers, 1928); O. S. Boucke, *The Development of Economics*
1750-1900 (New York: The Macmillan Company, 1921).

examining the structure and functioning of the institutions through which economic activity takes place," while Fairlie thinks of politics as dealing "with the life of men as organized under government and law, in what is known as the state." [12] In my *Political Power*, [13] I have undertaken to distinguish between the political and other social groupings.

It would not be far from the truth to assume that what many economists have in mind is the study of the phenomena of commodities and services having exchange value in a pecuniary system, and generally that of a "free market"; and that students of government have in mind human relations centering around a frame of community organization in which group protection, order, justice, general welfare, integration loom large.

The government never attempts to regulate everything, or to leave anything entirely alone. Nor is the economic system ever indifferent to the political, least of all in military or civil emergency. The government does, ideally, [14] what can most effectively be done through the agencies and instrumentalities called political for the advantage of the community. The breadth and depth of this domain of behavior varies widely from time to time. Group defense, internal order of a type, internal justice of a type, emergency action, community advantage of a type varying with the technology and the ideology of the time—these are functions found in the care of the political agency.

There never was a "pure" economic order, any more than there was a "pure" political order; nor does one determine the

[12] John A. Fairlie, "Politics and Science," *The Scientific Monthly*, XVIII, 1 (January 1934), p. 23.

[13] C. E. Merriam, *Political Power*, p. 9.

[14] See C. E. Merriam, *Political Power*, chapter V, "The Shame of Power," for illustrations of the abuse of authority.

other except in the larger terms of the social order in which they both exist. Both contain regulative systems not operating without immediate reference one to the other, or with intimate interrelationship. There was never a system of free competition without political control, nor was there ever a political system, however autocratic it might seem, which did not provide for forms of individual liberty of consumption and production. In some tense moments, as in a desperate military situation, political power may seem to be complete in its absorption of individual activity, yet there are on the other hand moments when the individual may seem to be for the moment entirely free. But these are periods of highest tension or relaxation and they do not last long.

An understanding of these processes requires a closer analysis of the types of directives or controls which are employed in social action. When individual and social psychology are more fully developed, it will be possible to discuss this problem with far greater fineness of detail and far more penetrating understanding of the numerous interrelations involved. In the meantime we may proceed with the best available material, hoping that its very inadequacy may stimulate further and more perfect understanding.

Historical observation makes it clear that in times of sufficient tension the political is predominant—as in fire, famine, flood, plague, war. Much of social wastage reverts to the political, as the hungry, the naked, the sick, the aged, the helpless from one cause or another. At times these have been the care of the church and to some extent still are, but if no one else acts then the government is expected to "do something" about it. From this point of view the motto of the state might well be *Nunquam non paratus*. In any case there is religious consolation at the end of the road, if nothing can be done; and the rhythm and symbolism of the church provide the psychological basis of existence in impossible situations.

It is readily seen, however, that the control systems overlap at many points. The state also may employ the man; the state also may insure him against a wide range of contingencies; the state also deals with credits and currency in the most familiar fashion; the state also deals with transportation, with business codes; with education, recreation, health, welfare on a widening scale.

When we come to deal with modern types of organization, the nature of the competing controls becomes still more similar in nature. These are the large-scale or monopoly form of economic organization, and the quasi-public corporation.

In our day the trend is in the direction of larger units of activity, whether political or economic or both. The small feudal units gave way step by step in the face of enormous resistance to the larger combinations now termed nations. Impossible as it seemed at one time, there came to be a common flag over France, England, Italy, Germany, instead of a score or more banners. In the phase of sharpest tension, the political form was autocratic in design; but later the zoning of power became liberal in practice, although the theory of political centralization remained.

The trend in recent years, especially in the last fifty years, has been in the direction of larger units of economic organization. Units of production have tended to increase in size, until their budgets and their numbers of retainers are now greater than those of many smaller states.[15] All over the western world the older landlords have been replaced by the

[15] See A. A. Berle and G. C. Means, *The Modern Corporation and Private Property* (New York: The Macmillan Company, 1934).

rising leaders of industrial corporations in one form or another, until the nationalistic large-scale movement in politics is rivaled by the large-scale concentration in the economic field. Furthermore, as these industrial units grew larger and larger, they tended to take on the form and type of the political units which surrounded them. The structure, activities, control methods of a large corporation became more and more like those of the large political corporation. The more loudly laissez faire was proclaimed, the more rapidly did industry itself become organized.

In transition periods, indeed, some of the large and powerful companies have been given what would be called political powers outright in their concessions.[16] The old-time guilds were examples of this tendency to combine political and economic powers in striking fashion, and the later Merchant Adventurers were equally illustrative of the same practice.[17]

Even without such specific authorization, present-day industries in what are called "company towns" sometimes have taken over almost the whole power of government in such fields as taxation, police, health, housing, education, within or without the law as the case might be. These *de facto* controls, indeed, extended as far as cities, counties, and States at times. In Texas one whole county is a private county.

Within these large-scale industrial units, notable control

[16] See A. C. McLaughlin, *The Foundations of American Constitutionalism* (New York: New York University Press, 1932), chapter II, "The Colonial Corporation." W. R. Scott, *The Constitution and Finance of English, Scottish and Irish Joint-Stock Companies to* 1720 (Cambridge: The University Press, 1910-1912).

[17] W. E. Lingelbach, *The Merchant Adventurers of England* (Philadelphia: Department of History, University of Pennsylvania, second series, vol. 2, 1902) dealing with associations such as the Muscovy Company, the Levant Company, the East India Company. In this country the Virginia Company and the Massachusetts Bay were striking examples of this quasi-private, quasi-public type of organization. See H. L. Osgood, *The American Colonies in the Seventeenth Century* (New York: The Macmillan Company, 1904-1907). M. W. Jernegan, *The American Colonies* (New York and London: Longmans, Green and Company, 1929).

systems promptly appeared. The government of these units was not constitutional but autocratic in many instances. Individual liberty and enterprise were ruthlessly subordinated to the larger purposes of the new organization or those controlling it. The new captains of industry were able to say and did not hesitate to say *Go;* and *he goeth* was the answer.[18]

The control methods were simple enough: loss of employment; lower or higher wage and hours; the working conditions; delimitation of the range of the competitors, or their destruction, or assimilation; fixing of prices and quantity and quality of production; control of lines of credit—promises of affluence or threats of bankruptcy. These are old-time methods but when employed by the larger scale enterprises and especially by those in monopoly or near monopoly form, they became far more formidable than ever before. The process of mergers went on apace and the area and intensity of control grew greater and greater as time went on.[19]

The great company assumes many of the characteristics of what is commonly considered a government. It has a legislative body, an executive, an administration, a department of state (public relations), a law department, a treasury, of course. It takes on many of the characteristics of what is called bureaucracy. The heads are invisible and intangible or tend to become so; they lose contact with their men; personnel divisions spring up; security of tenure becomes an issue,

[18] Mr. Taft said: "The time came when it was possible in some great corporations for the officers and directors to issue with the same nonchalance and certainty of their being complied with, orders for steel rails or industrial equipment, on the one hand, or for the delivery of delegations in a state, county or national political convention, on the other."—*Journal of the National Institute of Social Sciences,* I, 1, 1915, pp. 64-65.

[19] See *Recent Social Trends in the United States,* Report of the President's Research Committee on Social Trends (New York and London: McGraw-Hill Book Company, Inc., 1933). A. A. Berle and G. C. Means, *The Modern Corporation and Private Property.*

leading the way to pensions and other forms of insurance. Inflexibility and worse may creep into the organization as it becomes strong, irresistible, and proud. Responsibility may be resisted and evaded. The irregularities often follow a strikingly regular pattern of attempted escape from central supervision by a large concern. Thus government thrust out of the front door ostentatiously comes in at the back door quietly.

With reference to their weaker rivals these great ones may lay down rules of action to which conformity is as important or perhaps even more so than compliance with the law itself. Manner and mode of production, prices, profits, areas of marketing—the whole gamut of production—may be swept by the benevolent supervision of the stronger. And the penalties may be swift and drastic—rivaling the death sentence in government in some cases where financial ruin is the alternative. Trials and executions are no less a phenomenon of industry than of government, and at times almost as publicly. Poverty, insanity, disgrace, the grave even, are in the train of the powerful who sit in the seats of economic government from time to time. More than one man has been sentenced to hari-kari by the decree of a financial board or boss who showed him the way out. The characteristics of the shame of power are repeated in a close view of many of the operations of industrial enterprise.

Nor can it be forgotten that in these same hands there rests at times direct political authority. Orders may be issued for action or for inaction through the political boss, if there is one, or through the governing agencies whomsoever they may be, under certain conditions. These economic governments spread out over the whole field of business enterprise and even reach into the most remote corners of the earth. As

ruthlessly as government they invoke their power and penalties against the recalcitrant in the attempt to integrate and
organize authority in a given domain. If they cannot tax,
they can fix prices—and perhaps escape taxation themselves.
If they cannot fine, they may weaken or ruin even more
effectively. If they cannot imprison they can deprive of employment and drive the weaker toward starvation. If they do
not raise armies, they can organize their own deputies into
coal and iron or other police and carry on struggles in times of
industrial strikes—little short of civil war in some instances;
and they may also control the local organization of force and
justice, or intimidate, if not own.

They may control the working conditions and hours of
thousands of men, and, privately, shall we say, regiment their
conduct to an extent not equaled by the organization known
as the government. Especially under the decentralized political system of the United States, they may assume and
exercise wide and little restrained authority over the lives and
fortunes of men; and when the life span or working span is
over, they are legally free of responsibility for the future of
the crushed, broken, or aged.

This may not involve the process of direct corruption at
all, but the irresistible pressure of organized fluidity of gold,
where its claims are dominant. Rulers alone do not possess
the veto, which may be found in other hands as well; nor is
the power of appointment always where it seems to be.
Curiously enough, a corporation may obtain powers under
the laws of some States, giving greater powers than the State
government itself may exercise.

Furthermore, the relations between these larger units
themselves become a problem of far-reaching importance to
the community of which they are a part. Great "companies"

may struggle and make war with each other within the boundaries of the State, as railway groups, or steel groups, or oil groups arise and contend for the mastery. At the same time comes battle with the smaller companies, concerns, and individuals, and the pressure of all of them upon the consumer and upon the worker and upon the state itself. These acute struggles create new types of tensions which the government may be called upon to regulate in one fashion or another. As these clusters of interests become national or even international in form, the problem of a control system becomes even more grave and even more insistent in demand for some solution. The conflicting groups at one time denounce and resist the state and at another call loudly upon the state for help in the establishment of some form of regularization and order. Thus railroads at one time ask for governmental grants of land; at another resist governmental regulation; at another ask for governmental loans; and again may attack bitterly the process of state regulation.

Here is an illustration of the interchangeability of political and other forms of control, showing how in a transition period with swift and unexpected developments one dynamic element may take possession of the vital forces of social direction and control. The degree of energy seemed to determine the situs of effective control, under whatever name.

From another point of view the quasi-governmental corporation takes on many of the characteristics of what might be termed private government. [20] On the border line between governmental government and industrial government, this

[20] Harold A. Van Dorn, *Government Owned Corporations* (New York: Alfred A. Knopf, 1926). Marshall E. Dimock, *Government-operated Enterprises in the Panama Canal Zone* (Chicago: The University of Chicago Press, 1934). Herbert Morrison, *Socialization and Transport* (London: Constable and Company, Ltd., 1933). B. E. Lippincott, *Government Control of the Economic Order* (Minneapolis: The University of Minnesota Press, 1935).

special form assumes something of the characteristics of each. While under the ultimate control of the state, it is meantime released from some of the ordinary accountabilities of regularly organized departments of government. This is notably true of personnel requirements and of fiscal supervision, which are designed to offer a higher degree of flexibility than is common and to avoid the difficulties arising from detailed statutory outlining of powers, or from omission of powers needed in unforeseen situations.

Through these agencies it is possible to cover considerable ranges of activity in which various types of controls or management may be used, especially in governmental experimentation with borderline phases of enterprise. Innumerable varieties of these hybrid types are constantly springing up especially under modern industrial conditions, although, as already indicated, they were familiar institutions centuries ago. The London Passenger Transport Board, the Tennessee Valley Authority, the German Kohlenparliament are examples taken from different fields, but all illustrating the same principle of combining semi-governmental, semi-industrial powers in novel forms of organization.

Just as the various types of federalism in government drove the orthodox commentators into hysterics in the effort to tuck them into old-time classifications into which they did not fit, so these new industrio-political associations are anathema to many students both of government and of economics, since they cut across the established patterns of behavior in these separate disciplines. To some, indeed, these unusual forms of organization seem as if born under the bar sinister, illegitimate offspring of some unlawful alliance, but to the student of government they appear as natural products of transition periods in which various forms of control are applied to emerging situations. No more remarkable than that the head of a family should at the same time be head of the village, or that the head of the state should be the head of the church, or vice versa.

It is not the name of the structure that is important as much as the nature of the function it performs in the given social *entourage*. When a fire breaks out and threatens, no one cares whether the rescuer is a fireman or a volunteer, providing he does what is needed at the moment; in like manner few care whether a job is furnished by a public official or a private philanthropist, provided the need is adequately met.

This is as true of all associations as it is of the state. Resistance to group action fades with the recognition that a serious need is being satisfied by the group effort in question. If the pangs of hunger or fear or desire become sharp enough, the intermediation of the church or the family or the economic group or the state is little resisted. The sense of need paves the way to acceptance of ministrations otherwise unwelcome; makes the priest, the doctor, the banker, the governor a welcome guest where otherwise he would find the door barred.

If we look at the problem of control, political or otherwise, in any cycle of development of a power pattern, we find continually at work opposing tendencies as to extension and contraction, whether in state, church, or guild. If this were not true the group would soon become all center and no circumference, all the mechanism of regulation and nothing to regulate. The rationalizations of these alternating movements will, however, be based on obviously partial views rather than a total view of the functional situation—even within the group. Individuals and clusters of them will resist the control action of the group by appeal to "basic principles" which they will assert are more fundamental than the alleged purpose of the projected action of the group—state or otherwise. In like manner the rationalization of the power group will be based on a partial view of the total situation, and will appeal to basic principles of associated action, political or otherwise.

Even within this field there may be further divergence of opinion as to whether the proposed line should follow the pattern of the political, the ecclesiastical, the economic. And extensive argument and pressure in one direction or another will ensue. Should the poor be cared for by the state or left to the mercies of the church; or should we rely upon the impelling force of hunger and perhaps the survival of the fittest, in Darwinian language? These are the questions that arise daily in the adjustment of competing control patterns. Freedom and order are the slogans most commonly used, while justice and mercy follow at a respectful distance.

The student of government has no quarrel with these pressures and counterpressures, confusing and even irritating as they appear at times; for they are the essence of the political equilibrium itself. If no pressure existed it would be desirable to stimulate it, and if no centripetal or centrifugal pattern appeared it would be equally desirable to construct one.

The chief excitant is some dynamic change coming with some new factor within the group or without.[21] Such a factor may be discovery, invention, mechanical or social, some flaming idealism, some extraordinarily forceful personality, some attractive ideology; or pressure from without in the form of war, invasion, menace, the motor, Jerusalem—Napoleon, democracy, communism, imperialism. Any of these dynamics

[21] See chapter III.

may demand readjustment and reorganization. To this pressure the answer is some new pattern of control, which again may be political or otherwise.

The effort of the struggling, writhing mass of a given society at a given time to reorganize and readjust itself for safety, comfort, or convenience may hit upon a wide variety of forms, political, economic, or otherwise. But the development of the patterns of social control cannot be understood if too wide a difference between types is assumed, as, for example, between the economic and the political. The assumption that such a gap really exists has been responsible for much of the current confusion in thought during recent years. It has tended to push the discussion of proposed programs away from their social utility, over to the slippery and insecure query as to whether the proposal is essentially "economic" or essentially "political" in nature, with assumptions that are not in either case warranted, and with practical consequences that may be tragic.

Thus the relatively simple problem of the ownership and operation of municipal street railways may become the center of a furious storm in which public and private interests are placed in bitter opposition, when in fact solutions that are neither public nor private, such as the London Passenger Transport Board, are possible alternatives. On a larger scale the proposed socialization of all or sundry industries often leads into darkness and violence because of false assumptions regarding the inner nature of economic and political controls, and their presumed exclusiveness and incompatibility. The answer need not be a flat yes or a flat no, or a blind and costly struggle between reds and blacks. Of social, economic, political forms and processes it may be said, "there are as good fish in the sea as have ever been caught." Our social inventive genius is equal to the task of readjusting social and economic life to new influences, provided there is the will to undertake the task without too great prejudice against realities and too great a fear of change.

In the attempt to escape from feudalism the modern state set up an absolutistic and autocratic system through which the unit of operations was expanded from the outgrown small feudality to the larger territorial area we now call the nation state. It was found possible to establish the principle of trusteeship in this new unit, after prolonged democratic struggles, and to institutionalize the responsibility of ruler to ruled. It is equally possible to adapt this larger territorial area and its group machinery for control to the changing industrial situation now confronting it. This does not involve the disintegration of the political association but its more facile adaptation to the changing conditions imposed upon it by new devices mechanical and social, and in forms not described in the older terminology of juristics. When technological changes, such as transportation, communication, enlarged production upset either political or economic units, as they do, the sound answer is not violent opposition to change as such, but sharper efforts toward reorientation and reintegration of disrupted life ways.

It may be asked which of the competing control systems is superior or supreme. The long-range answer is any of them, in a series of phases of social development. In the higher range of value systems the religious groups assert their superior claims to understanding and authenticity in all periods; and at all times or many times in some individuals, and at some times in all groups their demands are given recognition and their interpretation of values accepted. In the wide range of human choices as to services and commodities the economic group has frequently asserted its superior claims to outstanding techniques of production and exchange, and from time to time and place to place, these claims have been recognized by the generality of the given community.

The group of techniques that can be brought together under the name of science and education have a set of values which they put forth for recognition, and from time to time they are rejected, postponed, and recognized. Likewise the group characterized as political presents a set of skills and a type of personnel dealing with various phases of human behavior, centering around a framework of order and justice; and the claims of this group are also recognized and validated by the acceptance of the bulk of the given community.

But in case of conflict, who then shall give the word of decision? Often there is no "decision," since the outcome is the equilibrium of forces in an integration, which includes them all. The development of such a balance is, indeed, often the function of the political—the equilibrator—the broader social frame of reference.

In conclusion it is plain that there is no historical or logical basis supporting the extreme claims of those who attempt to boycott the state as an unworthy social instrument, or to deify the state as the earthly lord of human destiny, or to decree priorities in competing controls. Neither the proposition that the state soils whatever it touches, nor the counterproposition that the state sanctifies and saves whatever it touches has any sound basis in experience or reflection. These are merely the battle cries of competing groups, having symbolic value rather than rational validity.

A sounder principle is that the role of various groupings, their techniques, personnel, values, the family, the state, the church, the industrial and the cultural, shifts with shifting trends of civilization from one period to another, with the types of pressure groups, the technologies, the value systems and behavior patterns of the times. In our own day the rapidity of social change and the urgency for new forms of social control place a heavier emergency burden on the state than in the preceding cycle of western development. But it must be noted that this involves a change in the broad framework of society, rather than in the fundamental function of the state. Other types of control may later develop more widely and more vigorously in the new framework set up by the now emerging twentieth-century society.

Militarization and demilitarization are functions of a tension situation known as war-peace; socialization and "desocialization," if there were a term corresponding to the reality, is a function of another alternating tension situation, sometimes called industrial war-peace. Unless we hold to the principle that the structure-function of government shifts with the technology, the ideology, the special tension of the time, we are adrift on a stormy sea without rudder or compass.

The basic troubles of our time are not fundamentally "economic" only, but are scientific and technological, territorial-racial, socio-political, philosophical-psychological. Our difficulties involve forms of behavior, value systems, ideas, and institutions beyond the bounds of "economics" in any ordinary use of the term. To characterize this bundle of factors as "economic," and then even worse to try to solve the problem in terms of old-time economics, is the supreme misunderstanding of our time. The organization of the old value systems and the new science in workable forms and practices is the root problem of the present age.

III
THE PHILOSOPHY OF PESSIMISM
AND THE
PRACTICE OF VIOLENCE

THE EARLIEST POLITICAL scientists sought for types of political society, perfect in nature and unchangeable in form.[1] One of the great problems of the Greeks was to protect themselves against an unstable equilibrium disastrous to their social order. In these early ideal states elaborate provision was made to prevent change of any nature in the ideal systems once set up. Plato went to the extent of supervising games and dances in order to guard against possible degeneration through the agency of rhythm—jazz perhaps or some other rhythms that must have been equally, shall we say, stimulating? The state must be set back from the sea coast to avoid demoralizing contacts with wandering sailors; the relations with other states should be reduced to a minimum; none should be allowed to go abroad until the age of forty and then to bring back only such reports as demonstrate the superiority of the ideal state over all other systems.[2]

It was not until two thousand years had gone by that the French political scientist, Bodin, recognized that the function of politics was not to prevent change but to render change as little wasteful as possible under the conditions. From this

[1] Kenneth Burke, *Permanence and Change* (New York: New Republic, Inc., 1935).

[2] See Plato's *Republic* and *Laws*; Aristotle's *Politics* for details of insurance against change.

time forth the adjusting factor of political science has generally been recognized. Marx might be cited as a possible exception, since he indicated that when the Marxian plan was
finally established—the classless society—there apparently
would be no need for change—certainly not for political
change—since in this society government comes to an
end.[3]

Constitutions of government even began to provide specifically for methods by which they might be changed in an
orderly fashion. The discussion now began to turn not on the
question whether governments change but whether this
change can be controlled by deliberate act of man, or whether
it must come in the slow course of history and through a
series of accumulating variations little dependent on any
human will. Edmund Burke debated this question with the
fiery American, Thomas Paine. The great German jurist,
Savigny, wrote a brilliant treatise on the codification of the
German law, in which he held that change must be brought
about not by legislation, but by the longer route of interpretation and application through the courts.

The outcropping of constitutions in western Europe put
an end to the question whether fundamental law could be
consciously shaped or altered, and a new era of conscious
legislation was ushered in all over the western world, continuing down to our own day as one of the characteristic
features of the time. It was a notable advance in political
thinking when it was finally recognized that the basic law of
the political society could be consciously and deliberately
altered by the will and intelligence of men. A century later it
is difficult to realize that any other position could ever have

[3] On the history of Utopias see Lewis Mumford, *The Story of Utopias* (New York:
Boni and Liveright, 1922).

been taken, but as we turn over the pages of the political theory held by many important persons and interests of that time, the old view stands out clearly. The brilliant French essayist, Count de Maistre, was typical of this opinion when he compared constitution makers to the builders of the tower of Babel.

There had been many changes in government before this, to be sure, but the specific characteristic of the new view was: (1) that changes could be made by reasoned act; and (2) that they could be made by representatives of the people. This was the beginning of modern planning in the light of social objectives.

But not only was it recognized that changes might be made deliberately in the fundamental law, but further that many changes might be brought about by the process of ordinary legislation. This was to be accomplished through the newly established representative bodies in various states. In some cases, as in England, the same body might change both the fundamental and the ordinary law. In earlier times much of the rulemaking had been the work of administrative agencies who promulgated various regulations in the name of the crown. As administration developed under the Bourbons, Hohenzollerns, Stuarts, these rules often took on the form of what we now call law, although technically they were sharply distinguished.

The range of modern legislation covers almost every phase of social and industrial life. While these legislative acts have met with violent criticism and opposition, the attack is now directed not against the impossibility of legislative change, as in earlier times, but against the particular areas invaded or the modes and types of legislative determination. Spencer denounced the Sins of Legislators, to be sure, and many others have leveled their attacks upon legislation,[4] and vigorous assaults have been made against the interference, invasion, intrusion of the state in private affairs. But in the main these arguments have been aimed at legislation dealing with property rights or privileges and not at the whole process of conscious legislation itself. Or attacks have been made upon democratic capacity for making changes skillfully and rapidly, or at elements of the representative organization as incapable of action.[5] And there has been advocacy of the superiority of executive or administrative decree, as in Germany and Italy in recent years.

In general it is taken as established, however, that important changes may be made by conscious action of the government, whether democratic, representative, or otherwise, as against the position that important changes must come only from the slow drift of time and custom. The very interests opposing legislation in one field advocate it in another, or even urge types of legislation in the forbidden fields, if they are aimed in the desired direction. Much of the recent legislation in the industrial domain is the result of pressure by industrialists, as in the case of types of banking and security legislation.[6] For example, a law to the effect that drawing of an overdraft is prima facie evidence of criminal intent was demanded by bankers; blue-sky laws by the investment bankers.

[4] See in particular W. E. Lecky, *Democracy and Liberty* (New York: Longmans, Green and Company, 1896). Emile Faguet, *The Cult of Incompetence* (New York: E. P. Dutton and Company, Inc., 1916).

[5] See Herman Finer, *The Theory and Practice of Modern Government* (London: Methuen and Company, Ltd., 1932), for review of chief considerations in this field.

[6] See C. E. Merriam, *The Written Constitution and the Unwritten Law* (New York: Richard R. Smith, Inc., 1931), chapter I. Herbert Croly, *The Promise of American Life* (New York: The Macmillan Company, 1909).

In the United States there was at one time a cult of the unchangeable constitution, arising curiously enough just after three basic changes had been made—namely, the Thirteenth, Fourteenth, and Fifteenth Amendments. The expression of a constitutional theory widely entertained was voiced by the distinguished jurist, E. J. Phelps, in his presidential address before the American Bar Association in 1879. On that occasion, he urged that constitutional questions be taken from the realm of general discussion and placed under the exclusive jurisdiction of the bar. Lawyers, he believed, should unite in "setting their feet upon and their hands against all efforts to transgress the true limits of the Constitution or to make it at all the subject of political discussion." The Constitution, he said, should not be "hawked about the country, debated in the newspapers, discussed from the stump, elucidated by pot-house politicians and dunghill editors, scholars in the science of government who have never found leisure for the grace of English grammar or the embellishment of correct spelling." In the meantime, however, important constitutional changes have been made and even unmade as in the case of the Eighteenth Amendment. Revolutionary changes have been made in taxation and suffrage, and undertaken in the domain of drinking habits—amazingly adopted and amazingly repealed. Obviously the amending clause of the Constitution is as much part of the document as any, and the formal amendments are as constitutional as the Constitution itself.[7]

Assuming, now, (1) that governments change, and (2) that change may be consciously designed and executed, we may proceed to consider alternative roles in social mutation.

[7] H. V. Ames, *The Proposed Amendments to the Constitution of the United States During the First Century of Its History* (Washington: American Historical Association, Annual Report for 1896), vol. 2, pp. 3-442.

How does it happen, we may ask, that in the moment of the greatest triumphs of intelligence, violence should assume so large a place in the making of important social decisions? How is it that in the moment of universal education, and on high levels of culture, such as that attained in modern Germany, this very intelligence has been forced to yield to the organization of force—by the substitution of dictates for discussion? And how does it happen that war cries and revolutionary slogans are sweeping around the earth, demanding that guns be accepted as the last word in social wisdom?

Did Marx's doctrine of violence as the way to economic change poison the world until the same idea was accepted by those who regarded him as anathema; or did he merely hit upon a fatal weakness in modern social organization and philosophy in advance of others? Or did he unwittingly take over the militaristic philosophy, and adopt the rules of the game of death?

An answer requires first of all an analysis of the conceptual background of the doctrine of modern violence, for its roots run back circuitously but surely to a series of associated fragments of political and general philosophy.

Down to 1800 the rational nature of man had been strongly emphasized by theorists, and the role of human consent as the basic fact in the formation and continuance of government. The consent of the governed was based upon the assumption that men were capable of agreeing to political arrangements. On the heels of what seemed a lasting triumph came, however, the development of doctrines of violence as the essential method of social and political change, and these ideas have spread for three quarters of a century, gradually pushing their way forward to widespread recognition. The intellectual factors contributing to this result may now be passed in review in order that the origin and destiny of this doctrine may be fully seen.

By the middle of the nineteenth century, after a protracted period of struggle, it had been fairly well established that the political association based upon might (*Machtstaat*) should be replaced by the political society based upon right and justice (*Rechtstaat*). The implication of this change was that human rights should be fully protected and that changes might be made in a constitutional or regularized fashion in which the bulk or a large part of the community should participate. This was not accepted everywhere, but generally in the western world.

One of the fundamental features of the new movement was the attack on the role of the human will in the organization of social relations. The other was the alleged superiority of violence to alternative methods of social or political change. These movements are not wholly separable, but for the purpose of this analysis may be so regarded.

If we seek out the origins of the present-day worship of violence as a solution of social problems, we find them in the Marxian theory, in the doctrines of Nietzsche and Sorel, in the flowering of the practice of the Nazis and the Fascists.

In the revolutionary movements of the seventeenth, eighteenth, and early nineteenth centuries there were many examples of violence, but theoretically this was limited to emergencies in which no other form of redress was available, and was not exalted to the dignity of a dogma to which one must subscribe under penalty of proscription intellectually.[8] The doctrine of Marx, restated somewhat by Lenin and

[8] In the following paragraphs I am indebted to Dr. H. E. Cohen for many suggestions and for the use of his manuscript on the subject of violence as a method of social change.

Trotzky, proclaimed the necessity of revolution as the means of establishing the dominance of the proletariat.[9]

The state in Marx's view is nothing but the organization growing out of class antagonism, an organization of force, for the purpose of repressing the workers. He proposed not merely the substitution of one state for another but also the destruction of the state itself in this curiously blended philosophy.

Marx himself seemed at times dubious about the inevitability of revolutionary activity, but in Lenin force is seen as "the midwife of every old society which is pregnant with the new," and even more "this conclusion is the chief and fundamental thesis in the Marxist theory of the state." In the end violence and force will disappear altogether as "the necessity of observing the simple fundamental rules of everyday social life will have become a habit."[10] In Trotzky the tempo is even faster and the tone more violent and even ferocious.[11] Individual acts of terrorism are repudiated in these doctrines, but the necessity of a general movement of force is maintained.

Apart from the bewildered philosophy of Marx and his associates regarding the nature of the state, more effective formulations of the doctrine of violence as a mode of social change have been made by others, notably by Nietzsche and Sorel.

In the system of Nietzsche, if the scattered and often contradictory essays of this brilliant German may be called such, violence and war are glorified. Not, to be sure, primarily as means of social change, but as factors essential to the

[9] V. I. Lenin, *State and Revolution.* Leon Trotzky, *History of the Russian Revolution.* This doctrine was not, of course, accepted by the social democratic movement in Germany and elsewhere.

[10] *History of the Russian Revolution*, p. 83 ff.

[11] Leon Trotzky, *Dictatorship vs. Democracy* (New York: Workers' Party of America, 1922), p. 7 ff.

maintenance of civilization. On the one side there is actual pleasure in causing others to suffer, he maintains.

Who can attain to anything great if he does not feel in himself the force and will to inflict great pain? The ability to suffer is a small matter. In that line weak women and slaves often attain masterliness. But not to perish from internal distress and doubt when one inflicts great suffering and hears the cry of it—that is great, that belongs to greatness.[12]

Living [says the philosopher], that is continually to eliminate from ourselves what is about to die. Living, that is to be cruel and inexorable toward all that becomes weak and old in ourselves, and not only in ourselves. Living, that means therefore to be without pity toward the dying, the wretched and the old. To be continually a murderer? And yet old Moses said, "Thou shalt not kill." Be robbers and spoilers, ye knowing ones, he exclaims, as long as ye cannot be rulers and possessors. War is an index of health, a time when "feelings of prodigality, sacrifice, hope, confidence, extraordinary audacity and enthusiasm" burst forth abundantly. War barbarizes and so makes men more natural—it is the sleep of the winter period of culture; man emerges from it with greater strength for good and evil.

Sorel's *Essay on Violence* was a discussion of the uses of violence in social movements of our day, but distinctly more in touch with reality than the Marxians, and more nearly affiliated with the principles and modes of action of the French syndicalists. Capitalism is declining, government is cowardly; and therefore the revolution might be much more conservative than is generally supposed. Indeed, important changes have been brought about in England by what he calls, and seems to dislike, "cunning." Violence as seen in strikes and demonstrations is useful in dispelling the stupefaction of humanitarianism, and leads on to the great day of the general strike when capitalism will finally succumb to the

[12] F. W. Nietzsche, *Joyful Wisdom*.

organized workers. Proletarian violence "is not perhaps the most appropriate method of obtaining material advantages, but it may save the world from barbarism."

But in general it appears that the realistic mind of Sorel was more concerned with the maintenance of the "myth" of a revolution than with its actuality. A threat of violence might serve as the means of keeping alive the defensive instincts of capitalists sufficiently to avoid a complete and premature debacle, and on the other hand as a means of keeping alive the spirit of the proletarian group, avoiding too great softness, too great timidity, too great a tendency in the direction of hypocrisy and futile compromise. Violence, following this line of reasoning, must be kept in the picture even though not employed in the wider sweep of an actual revolution, holding the various forces in line until the easy triumph of the workers when the state of economic evolution is completed. He wished to preserve the ethical admissibility of violence and the morality of revolution, even though recourse to it might be relatively infrequent.

The rise of the modern dictator brings a new defense of force. The policy of Hitler is directed toward the amplification of the role of violence and war as instruments of national policy; and this was evidenced in the internal "terror" and in the gestures toward other states while moving in the direction of rearmament. Underneath these more recent developments lay the philosophy of militarism, developed for a century particularly in Germany but with representatives elsewhere.

Mussolini once said:

And three cheers also for war in general. It is cursed in word and deed by a herd of bastards and fools and infinitely blind and ignorant multitudes, nevertheless, the adorable facts will not change their form and their onward march. War, a physical and spiritual fact combined, cannot fail to exist in a world in which everything from the act of thought to that of undertaking and accomplishing the slightest deed of free action, is a struggle and war against something or somebody.[13]

What is the basis of this cult of force? Sorel once said that pessimism and violence are happy companions. The violence of our day is not the result of savage determination to achieve a predetermined goal, but the outcome of defeatism. It is not fancy that has inspired these demonstrations but fear and frustration. They are blind blows at an unseen, unlocated, dreaded foe that pushes down until any form of action seems better than none—or than what seems like futile action. The confused and contradictory programs of these movements represent the confusion of the leaders and those to whom they appeal. The programs of Mussolini and Hitler have been the despair of those who undertook to analyze them and discover some inner element of unity, some central rational core from which a reckoning might be made to other points in some frame of reference.

They are consistent only in that they exhibit rage against what is, in emotional disturbance and upsurge, demanding an unknown something—a desire felt dimly but unformulated in any specific program—a feeling expressing itself first of all in forms of diabolism which turn against visible persons who may be built up as enemy figures—Jews, liberals, democrats, socialists, communists, Catholics—critics of any sort, or even those who remain neutral and in their neutrality and silence pass the severest judgment on rage and folly.

The root of this defeatism is sometimes traced, as in the case of Germany, to the late war, but in truth the origins of

[13] Quoted by H. W. Schneider, *Making the Fascist State*, pp. 259-260.

modern despondency go deeper down in modern history than this tragic conflict, however influential it may have been and undoubtedly was in deepening depression.

Curiously enough in the Marxian theory the old Calvinist position was restated, in other terms, to be sure. In theology the individual destiny was foreknown by God, but the individual might still struggle on, since he did not know what the Divine Intelligence knew. In dialectical materialism, so-called, he might discover that he was the "mirror" of reality only, although his understanding of his mirrordom did not change the inexorable movement of things to the inevitable end.

Further, the Darwinian theory was employed by some thinkers to demonstrate still more emphatically that the course of events is a blind struggle for survival of the fittest, and that the sweep of evolution is uninfluenced by what men may think, say, or do about it. In the Spencerian interpretation of this biological doctrine, the law of conduct and consequence is the basic law, and interference with it can accomplish nothing. If this were really true, it might of course be asked why the great Herbert should waste his time in railing against what in any event was a futilitarian gesture of impotent men. Others took up the survival of the fittest, consciously or unconsciously, and made of it a clash of force determining the outcome of human development, with reflection playing little if any part. Intelligence again was thrust far back to the rear and non-intelligence pushed to the front again as the presiding genius of our civilization.

In Germany especially, pessimism assumed a philosophical form which fitted in with some of the developments of the time. In Hartmann and Schopenhauer the will of the universe, speeding forward to the perfection of liberty, as Hegel had described it, became a blind force, itself unconscious of the where or why of human existence.

But how did it happen, one may inquire, that as man became more intelligent he became less "rational"? How did the greatest conquests over the dark continents of ignorance and superstition disqualify him for the exercise of his rational nature? By what *tour de force* was man at one and the same time emancipated from ignorance and enslaved by his own learning? How did he forge chains for himself as he cast off the fetters that nature had fastened on him for centuries? How did anti-intellectualism emerge from science?

The chief factors in this process were determinism of different varieties, materialism, pessimism, an interpretation of the survival of the fittest. Over against the high point reached by the social-contract school (seen in Kant) came the swing of the pendulum in the opposite direction. Determinism enveloped the individual will in the mazes of an outside environment—in the case of Marx an economic environment, in the case of Buckle and others a physical environment—which conditioned his way of life and his thinking.

The individual did not shape the course of things, but the course of things shaped him fundamentally; he did not create institutions; he was on the contrary created by them. He was only the reflection of their reality. In this sense he again becomes the pawn of fate or the external world however characterized, and his individual will and intelligence counts for little if anything, nothing in strict reasoning, as against the overwhelming forces driving him on and conditioning his every turn of behavior and thought. The climax of his "effort" [14] only reveals to him that he did not really make an

[14] See T. V. Smith, *Beyond Conscience* (New York: McGraw-Hill Book Company, Inc., 1934).

effort, since all that happened would have happened without him.

We may glance at the pessimistic philosophy of Schopenhauer, son of a banker and an actress, first published in his *World as Will*, in 1819, widely read throughout Western Europe and reminiscent of Napoleon. Hartmann's *Philosophy of the Unconscious* followed in 1869. The will in this philosophy is a perpetual desire to be, and this desire is the central point in all existence. But the will is also the origin of all evil, and it produces the worst of all possible worlds, instead of the best, as the idealists have contended. History is an unending drama of murders, robberies, intrigues, and lies; if you know one page you know it all. The more life is perfected the unhappier it becomes. "Laughter and tears are two peculiarly human phenomena." The final triumph of the will is not to will—renunciation of life itself. His particular antipathies were the Jews, Hegel, and the "professors of philosophy." The Jews will not renounce existence and therefore are the most immoral of all. The will of the universe is, further, unconscious will, blind and purposeless, drifting it knows not where.[15] It moves toward no goal, except as willing itself is an end.

The most recent expression of this general doctrine of pessimism regarding the outcome of events is Spengler, *The Decline of the West*, in which the decadence of our time is elaborated and the tragic outcome confidently predicted—less confidently since the Nazi development.

Not only is the intelligence of the individual discounted as a creative force, but the intelligence of the universe itself is unconscious and blind. If the human race were wise, it

[15] In Hartmann a new factor, intelligence, may direct the will not to will, which signifies the end of the world in universal suicide.

would arrange for a final day of universal suicide to end the tragedy of existence in this somber fashion. The systematic philosophy of pessimism had wide vogue for a generation and made its way often unconsciously into the thought of the period, contributing as it went to the weakening of the role of intelligence in human affairs, and still more to the degeneration of human hope. The climax of intelligence again is that there is no intelligence or will in the universe, only what seems so to the unintelligent intelligent.

The doctrine of the *un*conscious was followed at the end of the century by the doctrine of the *sub*conscious, which in a sense pushed the unconscious from the throne, we cannot say of intelligence, but of attention. With modern biology and modern medicine the physiological or constitutional basis of behavior became a center of inquiry and discovery. The long experience of physicians with the relation between physical infirmity and mental state, and vice versa, now began to expand rapidly with the aid of the new techniques and insights. The determining influence of the physical state upon the mental, the roots of abnormality in physical constitutionalism, the conditioning of behavior through physical controls—these began to take new form and meaning in the light of new discoveries. The study of the vegetative nervous system, the study of hypnotism and trance-like conditions by Janet and others led to a broader formulation of the subconscious as a significant and perhaps a determining factor in human behavior.

At the hands of Freud the unconscious basis of the constitution became the foundation of theories of behavior and of new types of therapy. The will of the Hegelians became the libido of the Viennese, and the Hegelian thesis, anti-thesis, and synthesis became the ego, superego, and id—now so

generally conjured with by the psycho-analysts and syn-
thesists. Ideas and acts are interpreted in terms, not of ab-
stract intelligence, but of indirect warnings of the subconscious, rooted in the physiology or in the social experience
of the individual, particularly in the early stages of his life.

There is indeed a type of determinism here based upon
the fixation in the very early developmental phase of existence, which draws the behavior pattern of later years (unless unfixed by an analyst).

While on the one hand this philosophy of life might well
take the turn of greater confidence in the reconstructive
ability of the race, on the other hand it often fitted in with the
trend toward a view of life as an essentially blind or preter-
determined process in which the creative faculties of individual or race were greatly reduced.

Thus Marx, the great Undetermined, made Economics
King. Freud, the great Unanalyzed, made Libido the King.
Instruments of Production and Reproduction—Stomach and
Sex—constituted the new Lords of Behavior.

In this connection there must also be considered the influence of the doctrines of biological determinism, in which
heredity plays the leading role. In the strictest interpretation
of this doctrine, widely accepted, the type of the individual is
set at birth, and must continue unmodified thereafter. He
cannot shape his own destiny since this is predetermined and
he can create only within the narrow limits of the type within
which his life span must move. This is the opposite of the
doctrine of environmental influence, but almost equally de-
pressing on the eighteenth-century theory of the rational
man and his freedom of will in the reconstruction of the
world about him. This may also take the form of racial determinism of many different varieties.

These factors discovered by intelligence, taken together, have had their effect on the role of intelligence in human affairs. As intelligence has discovered the laws of the social process, it has raised the question whether intelligence itself was bound by these same laws. In the moment of puzzlement and doubt the symbols of action, dogmatic and violent, have been seized by those less concerned with the truth than with the propaganda of the deed—the "madmen" Huxley terms them. More than that, even, they have proclaimed the superiority of "activism" over thought and have discouraged further speculation likely to interfere with the power pattern which has been proclaimed. Objectivity, the search for truth, become anathema. It is announced that we "must think with our blood." Or if these doctrines are not extended to the whole field of social affairs they are at least proclaimed in the domain of social inquiry as a means of preventing the projection of any types of thought not congenial to those in authority.

So it comes about that on the highest level of intelligence the human race has ever attained, intelligence as a guiding principle in social change is placed upon the defensive by the very civilization out of which it has emerged after long struggles against superstition and force. The tragic consequences of this to the progress of the race have not yet been measured. The timid may see the downfall of a civilization which rejects its own basic principle and returns to the violence and brutality out of which it crawled through centuries of effort.

IV
CONSERVATION AND CHANGE
IN POLITICS

A NOTABLE FACTOR in the field of social change was the appearance of the Darwinian doctrines. Here was a theory of growth in terms of evolutionary development—a picture of human life and indeed of all life, human and other, as a constantly unfolding process of adaptation, adjustment, mutation. Here was a revolutionary doctrine with widesweeping implications for biological study, for theology, and for social science.[1]

Two opposite interpretations sprang up in politics. One asserted the complete vindication of the doctrine of laissez faire and the other the validation of the political process as that of unending change. These opposing ideas are nowhere more effectively stated than in Spencer and Huxley.[2]

The doctrine of the survival of the fittest was employed to justify non-interference with industrial arrangements, and the whole classical economic theory was restated in terms of Darwinianism. What can be more futile, said Spencer, than to hope to advance by violating the most fundamental law of nature—that of the relation between conduct and consequence? Political puttering can do nothing more than block the way of nature, although just how it was possible for humans to block the natural course of evolution seemed difficult to discover. The strongest survive, and the fostering of

[1] David Ritchie, *Darwinism and Politics* (New York: Scribner and Welford, 1889).
[2] Herbert Spencer, *The Man v. The State* and in *Justice*. T. H. Huxley, "Administrative Nihilism," in *Methods and Results* (New York: D. Appleton and Company, 1893).

the weak only delays the inevitable triumph of the fittest. Even in Spencer, however, the significance of change was admitted, but it must be change of the "natural" order and not of the man-made kind.[3]

On the other hand the conception of history as a vast process of evolutionary change stimulated the imagination of the world, following as it did the titanic drama of the Hegelian dialectic which depicted the course of history as the progressive development of human liberty. The stability of institutions was no longer safely based upon time, custom, and status; they were henceforth subjected to the constant test of their validity in a special situation. Their sacrosanct quality was gone, and it was open to every rival group to envisage its own chosen type of social organization as an evolution—the evolution of democracy—of socialism—of aristocracy—of whatever you like in the light of the "irresistible trends of evolution."

Even more significant, however, was the conclusion now reached that man might direct the course of change within limits. It was argued that while on the lower levels evolution is an unconscious process, on the higher levels of human life it becomes a conscious process of adjustment, subject to the intelligent direction of men—an emergent evolution. The brutality and blindness of nature may be directed by the human intelligence, as pestilence, famine, plague, fire are controlled by mankind; and the wild forces formerly thought of as devils or evil spirits may be tamed to the service of man.

Instead of a theory of non-regulation on the part of the state or of society, we arrive at a theory of conscious control over the course of human evolution. Instead of the determin-

[3] In other parts of his work he discussed the transition from militarism to industrialism and from status to contract.

istic survival of the fittest, we may have the voluntaristic control over various lines of human evolution, through human contrivance and design—within limits to be sure. The permeation of this idea through human thinking was of monumental meaning, for it established (1) the normality of change in institutions, (2) the possibility of conscious socially directed change in institutions.

Coinciding with a period of incredible speed in technological change, and with the rise of democratic sovereignty, this new doctrine opened the way to new heavens and a new earth. It was not merely revolutionary in the usual sense of the term, as when we speak of a revolution in France, but revolutionary and radical in the sense that it went down to the bases of human attitudes toward social change. It was a revolution that went down far below the surface of ordinary conflicts—revolutionary as the doctrines of Socrates, of Jesus, of Galileo, of Columbus, in their respective times and areas of action.

The defenders of religion swarmed out only to discover later that it was possible to adopt this new idea instead of anathemizing it. Was it not conceivable that God had chosen this method of human development, and would it not be a limitation on His authority to declare that He could not organize creation as He would?

The contending forces have often forgotten in the heat of their controversy that evolution consists of conservation and mutation as well.[4] Science itself staggered at mutation, uncertain in the war of geneticists and environmentalists, still unable to identify the situations under which mutations take place, except in a general way. Upon this might turn in last

[4] See the discussion in *The Obligation of Universities to the Social Order* (New York: New York University Press, 1933).

analysis the control of mutation, and the limits of modifiability, ease of and resistance to change. That there are broad
ranges of modifiability has been shown in animal and vegetable alike. The biologist can turn the cock into a hen and
Burbank can grow unbelievable forms of vegetable life.

Leaving out of the question the finality of type forms, it
is clear that there are areas of modifiability in human nature
which may be discovered, and which vary in the degree of
their resistance to modification by nature or design of man.
There are processes of metabolism and processes of mutation,
of renewal and of variation. There are values which we wish
to conserve, some of them, or to modify. It is important to
consider then what elements in social organizations may
readily be changed, what elements are relatively permanent,
and what elements may be changed although with much
difficulty. It is perhaps more important just now to assume
that there are such differentials in modifiability and to agree
that they should be diligently sought in a given developmental phase of a society, than to set down universals applicable in all situations.

By way of illustration, it is possible to say that the bi-
sexual relation cannot be changed; that the law of divorce
may be altered with relative ease; that the complete abolition
of the family would be accomplished only with very great
difficulty in modern society.

It is comparatively easy to induce a modification in
church procedure; difficult to break up an existing ecclesiastical institution without great disturbance of the community
and large wastage of social energy; and impossible to suppress
religion altogether.

Neither in nature nor in human society is the essence of
mutation well understood, and "sport" individuals or "sport"

types may at any time emerge with startling consequences. But both in nature and in social relations progress has been made in the understanding of variation and in its manipulation within certain limits. The biologist, the botanist, the breeder may evince a high type of skill in the reorganization of types by conscious design and planned effort; and society itself has undertaken methods of management of one form or another, such as prohibition of marriage within certain ranges of consanguinity, the exposure of the weaker infants, prohibition of the reproduction of various types of defectives, devices of birth control, and encouragement of birth rate.

There is a range within which obedience may be secured by one who is giving commands. The leader can function effectively only within a set of predetermined and generally understood lines of authority, some of which are almost automatic in nature and others call for reflection before acceptance. In the old story the soldier of the Czar hurled himself headlong down (or offered to) while the soldier of France asked, "Is it for *la patrie?*" The lover went down in the arena braving the lion to recover his lady's glove but threw it in her face, indicating that the challenge was not acceptable or usual.

What are the limits of obedience in a series of situations, the student of government may well inquire. Obviously there are such limits even in the face of the most rigid and unquestioned discipline. The soldier will not desecrate the sacraments; or shoot his son or mother.

A political leader may live in the midst of incredible devotion and acclaim, but there are strict limits to this devotion which he may readily transgress, if he makes the wrong moves. The Greek ruler who feasted his subject and then informed the guest that he had been dining on his own son was one of these.

In simpler and less heroic pictures it is easy to observe the limits of commanding ability, and the patterns of compliance which underlie the seat of power. A volunteer leader at a rural fire issues a series of orders until he reaches the limit or encounters a rival; if he orders a rival knocked down and out, his command would fall on deaf ears. If he orders the father attempting to rescue his child to be shot, he will not be obeyed, but discredited and ignored at all points.

The doctor, the boss, the teacher, the mother or father operates with an assumed set of patterns of probable obedience which are the condition of his authority. Beyond these he not only does not advance, but he slips back and perhaps clear out. This is as typical of non-political as of political relations, and in the social hierarchy works with amazing and amusing results, as when servants are directed to do what is outside their set of recognized duties.

The state is in no different position from any of the other groups at this point: Its legal omnipotence is secure in the arms of the jurists who will validate legality; but the state's practical omnipotence is another matter. Here the humblest may upset the highest at times. Even the jurists have evolved the saving maxim that the law does not require the impossible, and the vast apparatus of equity has been developed to rescue the law from its harsher moments.

Or laws may be quietly ignored. The live world is full of dead laws technically still alive, but practically departed. The average American is amazed when his attention is directed to the number of laws and ordinances he violates in the course of a year. The ordinance against expectoration on the sidewalks was enforced in an American city on Tuesdays and

Fridays by police order. In prohibition days periodical enforcement and fine became a practical system of license well understood and accepted. In a city which licensed its bars even when the State law forbade bars, a smart saloon keeper decided not to pay. But to his chagrin he was promptly arrested, tried and—incredibly—convicted in record time— really convicted as a man who would not observe the general understandings regarding community policy upon this important point. The local jury of the vicinity, sometimes wiser than the Solons who make the law, tempers justice with mercy.

The political atmosphere is as full of holes as is the air in which the aviator navigates, or the sea of reefs and shoals for the sailor. The political navigator, who undertakes to chart a course must be as aware of these holes and shoals and currents; for they may wreck his fairest hopes if he ignores them. Infinitely more complex and delicate, indeed, is the value and interest system or systems through which the ship of state must wind its way.

The resistances to be encountered in a given phase of political development, the degree to which and the manner in which these resistances may be modified or overcome, the types and forms of coöperation or attraction to be found, these are the material which the statesman cannot ignore. They are indeed the essence of his contract. If there are inexpugnable resistances there are also incredibly easy lines of advance, if the moment and the point be seized with dexterity. Almost as in battle there are at times open places in the line through which advance might be made, if only they were known. Examples of this in recent American experience are the passage and acceptance of the selective draft law in the late war; the sudden collapse of national prohibition; the quick thrust of policies such as the Agricultural Adjustment

Administration in the New Deal. On the other hand the
soviets could not break up hand-shaking, public kissing, or
compel the right turn on the walks.

When Theodore Roosevelt proposed to remove the words,
"In God we trust" from the dollar he aroused a wild storm of
unexpected indignation, as did Cleveland when he ordered
the return of the Southern battle flags.

In many instances what seem like entrenched prejudices
fall before relatively light pressure, as in the case of prohibition; while in other instances a light line proves to have fatal
strength. In a rapidly changing situation, the cohesion or
superior attractiveness of social groups or classes is not as
great as is sometimes supposed by their leaders. Individuals
with high susceptibility to appeals may be pulled over mag-
netically into new fields wherein they find a new home for
their household gods of interest, ideology and symbolism.

In this way Wilson took over the German Americans;
Hitler invaded the group of toil in Germany and enlisted
members there; the English Tories took over MacDonald and
some of his campfollowers with the greatest of ease apparently; the British aroused the fighting enthusiasm of the
South Africans in the late war.

In these and countless other cases it is easy to see that
there are avenues of approach sometimes as broad and unexpected as the pitfalls and reefs.

Those who are concerned with political change may well
concern themselves with the un-formation of habits as well as
with their formation; for one is as vital as the other in the
great process of adaptation and adjustment. But precisely
here it is seen that habits are un-formed more readily by
persuasion, education, substitution, than by intimidation,
violence, and cruelty. The practitioner in plastic surgery uses

more plasticity than surgery, if he is skillful. As vegetation
thrusts itself up through the soil, it may carry with it for a
while the decay of the old, gradually pushing all aside and
coming into its own new position. There are, to be sure, cata-
clysms in nature as in human life, but wisdom controls many
crises and bends them to the purposes of human satisfaction
—all the way from birth to death.

The metes and bounds of modifiability are written large
in the records of many revolutionary movements and in
many abortive attempts at social change, whether by state,
church, or cultural group. We do not have, however, the
exact indices of modifiability, and herein lies the possibility
of deep-seated antagonisms in proposals for social alteration.

Unfortunately conservatism, presumably the official cus-
todian of conservation, does not deal uniformly with those
basic elements in social values and institutions which might
most advantageously be conserved. Conservatism often turns
to the defense of vested interests not functioning well and
hence requiring artificial reinforcement, such as slavery, or
serfdom, or modern industrial privilege. The very areas in
which change is indicated—the areas of decay—resist the
modification of the social pattern, surviving their functions,
projecting their prestige beyond their social utility. This
situation may be seen often in business, in government, in
church as well as in the state.

This is age lingering too long; it is power refusing to dele-
gate; it is privilege acting as judge of its own share of the
social dividend; it is the extension of the dead hand into
living relations. Thus conservation may find it necessary to
fight its way against conservatism, strangely enough. The
nation may defend its forests, its mines, its minerals, against
the special interests that waste them. Radicalism may be-

come the high protector of conservation—which might be conservatism in the highest sense of the term, and in its evolutionary implications. Likewise human resources vital to the future of the nation may be defended by the radical against the special privileged interest which seeks to exploit and waste them in the alleged name of conservatism.[5]

Conservatism might appropriately direct itself to the wisest ranges of modifiability, to appropriate rates and the wisest modes of change; but the practice is often quite different, amounting to a flat defiance of change impinging upon particular interests, even though the general interest may be advanced. So professional conservatism comes to be arrayed against conservatism in the broad sense of the term. This is conspicuous in the industrial world where business is often conservative in the sense of protecting vested interests, but intensely radical in ruthless change of machinery and organization in a limited zone.

Radicalism on the other hand may be found in opposition to social change indicated by the trend of the time, and may protect its own immediate interest as against the broader interest of the group and of posterity. It may reject the advance of mechanization; it may oppose the newer forms of industrial organization. Labor opposed the corporation originally as vigorously as capital opposed the trades union.[6] Unfortunately the social implications of invention have never been carefully scrutinized, nor has society adjusted itself to the displacement caused by new technologies, which help the race but ruin the individual worker affected.

Radicalism may confuse a value with a prejudice, as when the Marxians undertake the destruction of the state, fearing

[5] Lord Hugh Cecil, *Conservatism* (London: T. Butterworth, Ltd., 1928).

[6] See J. R. Commons, *A History of American Industrial Society* (Cleveland: A. H. Clark Company, 1910-1911).

it as an instrument of capitalism; or the anarchist attempt the destruction of education and science fearing it as the instrument of capitalism; or the overthrow of religion as the enemy of the proletariat; or labor-saving machinery, or modern production. A long catalogue of bourgeois practices were on the list of the soviets but later relinquished as hatred died down and a sense of proportion returned. It was proposed to abandon precedent in law as a bourgeois institution; to forbid dancing as a bourgeois institution; to taboo style as a bourgeois institution.

Radicalism resists useful social mutations, either because they are misunderstood, or because they do not fit in with the program of the group in power at the particular time. Radicalism may find itself at war with radical change, just as conservatism may find itself at variance with conservation.

The difference then in modern politics is not that between one group looking skeptically at all proposals for change, demanding great circumspection and prudence in change, and another group optimistic regarding possible change, and somewhat less critical as to the ways and means of change. These attitudes are not monopolized by either party in the social conflicts of our own or other days.

Not only are there many radicals in all conservative movements, but there are also many conservatives in every radical movement. The fundamental point of view of many conservative movements is the protection of elements which should not be conserved but modified. In less pronounced degree the attitude of many radical movements is not that of speedy recognition and incorporation of social mutations of a beneficial nature, but the limitation of mutations to those that are expedient at the moment for the group in authority. It is to be expected that those that are displaced or disinherited by science should resist until a way is found by which the gains of civilization shall not become a loss to them.

This is not a criticism of these movements, but an analysis of their relation to the great political and social problem of the relation between conservation and mutation.[7] It is in the nature of party movements that such compromises should exist in order that special groups may be satisfied and that parties may persist.[8] But it is important for those not at the core of these groupings, and even for those at their center, to have in mind the problem of conservation in its largest meaning, in order to preserve the critical judgment and choice which underlie all systems of general control.

Looking at the alternative forms of political change, past, present, and future, the chief competitors are violence, on the one hand, and invention with various forms of education, conciliation, persuasion, legislation, on the other.

Violence there will unquestionably be, for violence comes in when argument is at an end—for one party to the discussion at any rate. It is difficult to reason with unreason, and war is the organization of a situation over which reason no longer presides. The gains of civilization may be and are appropriated to the uses of warriors, as in the employment of the skills of chemistry and propaganda, but these skills are concentrated behind a blow at the will of an enemy, designed to force him to a course of conduct against his reason, judgment, and will. Such situations are likely to occur and recur both within and without the state. One person or one party alone

[7] John C. Merriam, *The Inquiring Mind in a Changing World* (Rice Institute Address, 1934). T. V. Smith, *Creative Skeptics* (Chicago: Willett Clark and Company, 1934).

[8] See C. E. Merriam, *The American Party System* (New York: The Macmillan Company, 1922).

cannot prevent them, since it is one of the peculiarities of violence and war that one party may invoke this form of decision whether the other likes it or not. We must then accede or resist, when the boundaries of reason are reached, or when an existing legal order and mechanism for justice are challenged and repudiated.

All rulers are on notice that this may occur at any time, within or without their domain. They may conceivably accept the solution involved in non-resistance, but this is unlikely in view of the nature of group organization and cohesion. The conquered, it is true, have often overthrown their conquerors, as in Rome, China, and India. Yet this alternative solution seems on the whole unlikely and ill-adapted to the nature of political organizations with which we deal here. A cultural or religious group might be more disposed to assert its cultural qualities of endurance than the governmental or the economic.

Alternative methods of social and political development have advanced at a rate far faster, even seemingly ineffective at times. Great changes of the last century have been caused by other types of stimulus than war. These alternatives are as follows:

1. Science and technology
2. Education
3. Persuasion—conciliation—legislation

A look at the social landscape of any western nation shows at a glance how profoundly social life has been affected by technological devices regarding transportation, communication, production, medical care. Pestilence and famine, two of the historic curses against which human hope and effort have been directed, are practically eliminated, while fire and flood have been greatly diminished and their losses greatly reduced.

It would be useless to organize a grand parade of all the great inventions of the last hundred years, but the impressiveness of such a series must not be forgotten in appraisal of the types and modes of political change in our time.

The influence of the evolutionary idea was concurrent with the rapid development of science, and especially with the amazing triumphs in the world of machine technology. The recent march of invention is one of the most impressive of all the pictures in the gallery of the human race.[9] Communication, transportation, quantity production, developed at a rate and in directions staggering to the imagination even of contemporaries. Tradition in this field is cast to the winds as older forms crumble and are cast aside. In this area of human activity there is no boasting of the fact that a machine is old but that it is the newest and latest to be found; no proclaiming that a process is ancient but quite the contrary that it is the latest. Industry accepts here the implications of a period of change and throws itself eagerly into the exploitation of the work of the scientists and inventors who made possible the newly developing industrial accumulations.

Scientific intelligence laid the foundations of modern prosperity, as well as of modern ideology. But industry often accepted the material basis while rejecting the ideological, using one for purposes of profit and the other, often an older ideology, to prevent adjustment to changing conditions.

It cannot be too strongly emphasized that the builders of modern civilization are the discoverers, scientists, and inventors. It was their initiative that made the wonders of the modern world.

Our civilization has been built not primarily by the

[9] On inventions see W. F. Ogburn in *Recent Social Trends*, chapter III.

warriors or by the entrepreneurs, but by the technicians, whose intelligence has penetrated the hitherto unknown and brought forth hidden treasures for mankind. The discoveries of the human mind, furthermore, are not accidental out-croppings, but the result of a high mental plateau attained by the human race after centuries of effort. They represent the possibilities in an era supplying scientific education, public order, and displaying keen interest in the outcome of scientific inquiry on a large scale—of a civilization which is essentially non-traditional, irreverent, imaginative, and bold on its material side, however it may cling to the opposite set of traits on the other.

These technological changes have been far more revolutionary in their immediate effects and in their wider implications than the bloodiest revolutions of any time. They have multiplied the productivity of the soil, the output of factories, given the hand one hundred times its former power, opened out materials and processes of incalculable value to millions of persons; and opened the way to a wonderland of achievement in health and well-being. In their immediate channels they have swept aside superstition, prejudice, misunderstanding, ignorance, sometimes with little and again with much resistance, but with the inevitable conclusion emerging.

The distribution and application of these gains of civilization is another story full of sorrow for millions of the disinherited, but the accumulation of vast riches for the race is incontestable.

The lag between what might be and what is, technically, is one of the tragedies of the time, but the piling up of the treasure heap is beyond doubt a fact with which politics must deal. I pause only to emphasize the sometimes forgotten truth that change involves not merely redistribution of what is, but the vast expansion of what is into far more. It is within the scope of government to reckon with this basic fact and to express it in realistic forms.

Education is a means through which political change may be effected, including in this the processes of the press, daily and otherwise, and the radio, the cinema, or other modes of intercommunication. This is now recognized by whatever group of bandits come into power, since they snatch at the schools for the propagation of their point of view, and at the press and the radio as similar instruments of obtaining conformity. At times it may seem as if madmen had taken possession of the schools, and were attempting to impose their will through the intelligence of the apparatus there established. Whatever their motives and whatever the degree of their success or failure in the long run, here is a speaking proof of utility of the educational system as an instrument of long-time and relatively peaceful change. Both the momentary morale and the long-time level of efficiency are determined by the quality of the schools; and this is now an accepted fact in all systems of power. Dictators, or others, may destroy or cripple their system by using it for the purpose of looking backward rather than around and forward— by employing schools as an agency for inculcation of tradition alone rather than as an agency for constructive and creative types of stimulation. But this is cutting down the tree to harvest the apples. [10]

The scope, direction, method, and speed of change in social and economic relations are determined by the cultural level of education and science. A war may speed up changes about to be made at the time, but the educational system deter-

[10] See K. S. Pinson, *Bibliographical Introduction to Nationalism* (New York: Columbia University Press, 1935).

mines the long-time preparedness for changes of any sort, and out of its group come many of the leaders in invention and adaptation.

Many far-reaching social and economic adjustments are effected through the instrumentality of legislation and accommodation in one or another peaceful form, and no period in the world's history has been more fertile in such changes than the last hundred years which may be called the golden age of legislation. Great codes have been built up without particular invocation of the sword, as earlier the Solonian Code, the Justinian Code, the common law, and much of the old Germanic law.[11]

Social legislation in all western countries during the last hundred years has wrought sweeping changes in the personal and property relations of millions of people, and that without a blow. The doctrine of laissez faire has been unable to stand against the flood of legislation sweeping down from a thousand sources with a steady pressure that could not be resisted for long. In the United States alone within the last generation the voters have been almost doubled, unlimited income taxation has been authorized, social-security legislation enacted—all within the framework of the law.

In Germany, Sweden, England, and other states far-reaching systems of social insurance have been put into force through the legislative method. Sanitary and housing legislation has been widely enacted. A wide variety of regulatory methods for the control of industrial practices have been enacted. Land-tenure systems have been modified; banking

---

[11] See James Bryce for comparison of these systems in *Studies in History and Jurisprudence* (New York: Oxford University Press; London: H. Frowde, 1901). Sir Frederick Pollock, *The Genius of the Common Law* (New York: Columbia University Press, 1912). Roscoe Pound, *The Spirit of the Common Law* (Boston: Marshall Jones Company, 1921).

and credit systems basically changed. Indeed an enumeration of the breadth and variety of types of legislation would constitute a review of almost every phase of recent social life. So numerous are these changes that Sorel himself comments on what he calls the cowardice of capitalism and its "dangerous" tendency to compromise rather than to enter upon violent ways of settlement. His encouragement of violence was intended fundamentally to offset the compromising tendency of the powers that be, in the fear that the present generation might become too much interested in progress through legislation. [12]

Invention is often an inducement to political change, but if this is technological invention, it may escape the notice of the powers that be, except as it may cross the path of some social taboo of the day, as did Galileo in his time or Darwin in his day. There is every reason to believe that scientific discovery and invention will sweep on in an increasing flood in the period before us, and that they will precipitate changes basically affecting the stability of particular holders of political power. Transportation and communication do not appear to be unconstitutional at any point or unpatriotic, but nonetheless they may be overturning the ancient landmarks as no enemy could possibly do; or they may be modifying the basic controls over human behavior in ways that would be denounced, if they were known.

What should a type of statesmanship opposed to all change and wishing to sanctify the *status quo* find it useful to do? (1) It should prohibit all scientific invention and discovery of every sort, and limit itself to the exposition of what is already known. (2) It should require all new ideas as to

[12] Marx in his earlier phases held that in certain countries like England and the United States basic change may be made without revolution. These are, it happens, the largest states with the longest experience in self-government.

social, economic, or political change to be registered and licensed, with ample provision for the revocation of licenses and appropriate penalties to be inflicted upon the licensees. (3) It should forbid the importation of unlicensed ideas or inventions from the outside, and establish a rigid and effective quarantine against them. And (4) it should further as far as possible avoid contacts with other states, assuming an attitude not merely of economic but of cultural isolation. But even then this hermit kingdom might find itself attacked by some outside power with modern devices and be overwhelmed in the new clash. Concurrent statesmanship would indeed be a prerequisite to the successful carrying out of such a program so that scientific discovery and invention might be forbidden throughout the world. But this itself would be an innovation perhaps equally startling in its implication.

It seems more probable that governments will increasingly lend their support to scientific discovery and invention rather than to its suppression. This is a condition of survival for the local group and of happiness for the world as a whole. Even the most enthusiastic advocate of the beneficent effects of violence would not wish to forbid the growth of scientific invention, for after all only through thinkers can we hope to utilize new discoveries in the effective organization of violence. New guns, new gases, new explosives, new robots of death can emerge only from an environment of invention, experiment, and reflection.

In the broad process of political change there is a heavy burden on the brokers and adjusters of social inventions, and on the roles of education, conciliation, administration, flexible statesmanship which will interpret the new to the old and prevent the moments of tension out of which may emerge the clash of violence.

One of the greatest needs of our time is the organization of our modern intelligence in terms of understanding of material inventions in their relation to social inventions. The wide gap between the understanding of machines and of social mechanisms is one of the greatest danger points in our civilization. The farther and the faster one advances without the other, the greater the degree of risk. Furthermore, as danger comes on, the mind trained in machines but not in social mechanisms recoils in panic and turns against all forms of social change, falling back upon the traditional and unchanging as a port of security, at the very moment when it has been rendered untenable by the new forces of invention and discovery. The next step in this *non sequitur* is to employ violence to repress changes necessitated by science. Thus tear gas is employed to break up freedom of discussion about some point raised by the modern scientific trends and producing a problem such as unemployment. When any tension arises from the failure to assimilate the old to the new, the recourse is likely to be to violence, conspicuously seen in the cases of Russia, Italy, and Germany. In other nations there is a strong tendency to use violence and repression to prevent even the discussion of the elements of an unpleasant problem, or the presentation of alternative modes of procedure. There may be governmental action or mob violence hurled against a new idea; and if this sentiment rises high enough and spreads far enough it is true that the only way out is violence again in one form or another, as seen in Germany and threatened in France by the Cross of Fire and other like organizations.

We are thus far unable to break the dangerous circle of mechanical invention—social distress and need of readjustment—social invention—panicky fear and return to tradition and then violence.

Machine mining in coal—distress—proposed socialization —resentment and appeal to tradition—violence and repression—this is the tragic cycle of our day in other than coal fields, over the wide range of industrial and social reorganization.

In many instances the organized agencies of political and social change are adequate to deal with these emergencies, but these governments rest upon the assumption that the bulk of the community is oriented to political change, and that agreement may be obtained upon the fundamentals of such change. Even a small minority bent upon violence may force counter violence and precipitate a state of civil war, as indeed happened in Germany. The far more flexible political arrangements of the British made it possible to ride the waves even of the general strike of 1926 in which internal conflict seemed for a moment unavoidable.

Severe tension, over-suggestibility, under-sophistication, lack of serene types in political leadership or appreciation of them; these are the formulas of disorder, in any community. These are the indices of change that will be turbulent rather than steady in its movements, adolescent rather than mature, with bitterness and blows at its center, rather than good will and conciliation—the work of what Huxley calls the "madmen."

In the long view of political science, the storm of violence dies down, and the warlike scowl of conquering Mars fades into one of deep anxiety as to what to do next. The battle has been won, and the blood sacrifices have all been offered. The prisons are full, and the *émigrées* are on the march. What now? Why not more gas, more machine guns, more steel and noise? No. The program? Experts are now smuggled in by the rear entrance, the task of reconstruction begins; life goes on again—the life of reproduction of social types and the life of variation and mutation. The task of compromise and conciliation begins again within a new frame of reference perhaps, or perhaps not even that, for within the inner circle there will not be unanimity but divergence, differences, discord that may flame out in counter violence.

The argument against force is not against force as such, but against the exaltation of a technique which is an admission of social failure to use other and better means of adjustment. Violence is the capitalization of a series of social omissions and errors, of unreadiness in the fields of social and political endeavor. It is not a diet but a drug.

Every war is the starting point of another series of traditions, perhaps imperishable in the memory of the group, but at the same time likely to be a type of tradition that will inhibit change and readjustment, and perhaps precipitate for this reason another cycle of disorders with the ultimate solution of violence again. New symbolisms are set up and to them appeal is made against whatever adjustment the symbol holders may judge unwelcome.

We may ask the question, What are the types of change most likely to be considered by governors in the period into which we come? These changes will, of course, be the result of variations in technology, in social invention and control, in social directives.[13] New machines for controlling our physical resources, new modes of remaking men, new patterns of social invention seem to lie on the horizon, assuming that our civilization does not bog down of its own weight in the

[13] An interesting résumé of such predictions is found in *Today and Tomorrow*, covering the future of science (Haldane and Russell); of man (Schiller); of morals (Joad); of women (Ludovici); of Darwinism (Brain); of biology (Jennings); of intelligence (Lee); etc., in some fifty small volumes (New York: E. P. Dutton and Company). See also H. G. Wells, *The Shape of Things to Come* (New York: The Macmillan Company, 1933).

swamps of violence and strife. It would be impossible and indeed an impertinence to undertake to say what the future contains in the apparently inexhaustible fairyland of control over natural forces.

The finger of science does not tremble as it points in the direction of conscious control of evolution—the triumph of intelligence in human relations, and the types of change growing out of this process are fundamental to all political speculation and programing.[14]

In the rational control of the processes of political change lie some of the richest possibilities for the human race, and at the same time some of its blackest dangers. Those who wish to accept the cult of violence may find on the pages of history enough of fire and sword to occupy all their reading hours and confirm them in their conviction of the inevitability and priority of violence in social change.

But a student of government will indicate alternative possibilities while not denying war and riot their relaxation in volcanic hours of smoke and death. In tension moments the scientist will inquire:

What are the chief points of tension and torsion

What are the strong points in the old system as it has developed and what are its weakest spots

What are the types of change best adapted to this particular phase and form of political development

What are the feasible programs of reorganization

What are the ways and means of fitting mechanical and social inventions into the old value systems and patterns of action

I am not saying this will be done; only that it could be

---

[14] On this point see E. G. Conklin, *The Direction of Human Evolution* (New York: Charles Scribner's Sons, 1921).

done. I am not saying what persons are competent for this task in a given society, or that their conclusions or suggestions would be generally followed. I merely state that there have been such types of change; and that the dicta of political science point in this direction. Certainly those who prefer blood and swords can find plenty of sharp swords in the world ready for their purposes and plenty of youthful blood ready to be shed in encounters of sundry sorts. There will always be streams of red blood, acres of soft flesh, mazes of sensitive nerves for those who can read the auspices of fate only in human entrails. I have no desire to wish away the obstacles to advance, but, on the other hand, I do not wish to shrink back from a hard task. It is even possible to combine a soft heart with a hard hand—provided that the head is not too soft.

V

STRATEGIC CONTROLS

IN ANY GROUP the regulative and control system may be
looked upon as a set of social directives, resting upon a
balance of forces, and implemented by certain mechanisms or agencies of organization. These live in an atmosphere
of understandings as to the range of control, the type of
control, the direction of control, and as to the personnel of
control. Without these general understandings there is no
organization, but only an unrelated mass of persons. The
quantum of power in political systems does not vary as
widely as is often supposed. The lines of association and authority change from time to time, shifting the form, however,
rather than the substance of control.

This is as true of any group as of the political. The inner
systems of social direction rest on strategic lines of integration which are essential or deemed essential to the given stage
of development of the given group. The location and interrelation of these lines and their continuing readjustment is an
inner problem of organization, political and otherwise. It is
the grand strategy to which tactics is subordinate.

This is the point at which the statesmen, using the term
in its broadest sense to include those in the inner circle of
responsible direction, rise or fall, as they do or do not identify
these controls in changing periods and interpret them to their
respective associations. If nothing ever changed, governance
would be relatively simple, as simple as guiding a ship across
an unbroken surface of water. It is the winds, tides, reefs,
shoals, storms that develop the art of the navigator, to say

[103

nothing of mutinies and pirates. Even the most exhaustive knowledge of the stars will not save the captain, if he does not reckon with these sailing hazards.

What then are these strategic control points? The problem is difficult, for the reason that the political situation is a moving equilibrium, a continuous reintegration or reorganization of changing factors, working not only from within, but also from without the group. The task of the statesman is to know the nature, strength, direction of these factors, how they may be modified, interrelated, brought together in some working pattern on some level of concurrence where order and justice may be achieved.

He must reckon at all times with elements in human behavior patterns which are fairly constant, and also with forms of change. Some changes penetrate the body politic so slowly as to be imperceptible, and others fall tempestuously with shattering violence, as in revolution from within or invasion from without. In his brilliant essay on *Technics and Civilization*,[1] Mumford has indicated some of the historic pitfalls which have entrapped the governors of times past and present. Whether his classification into eotechnic, paleotechnic, and neotechnic is the last word or not—probably not—he suggests types of changes which are often fundamental to the political patterns with which we now deal.[2]

The invention of a new weapon of warfare or a new device of warfare, the discovery of a new world, the invention of a new machine, the rise of a new ideology, the birth of a new idealism; any of these factors may so modify the life situation of a group as to compel reorganization of the patterns of control.

[1] Useful bibliography on pages 447-474 of Lewis Mumford, *Technics and Civilization* (New York: Harcourt, Brace and Company, 1934).

[2] W. F. Ogburn, *Social Change* (New York: B. W. Huebsch, Inc., 1922).

To illustrate, many of the most bitter and prolonged controversies have centered around changing situations on a predatory level, as in wars for territorial boundaries, or wars between conflicting racial groupings.[3] In China for long periods strategy centered around the adjustment of familial relations to the pattern of the state, with land and population control inseparably involved in this area of effort. In India the construction of castes lay at the basis of the system, and this in turn was profoundly affected by religious patterns of belief and behavior.

The Roman political powers concerned themselves with civil and military administration and with law—social inventions in which they made amazing progress and with which they achieved vast success. The medieval power systems centered around religious controls over human behavior, depending on authenticity of prestige and on facility in administration, broken through by the local feudal system and the bold claims of the shadowy Holy Roman Empire. Significant control points in later times centered around serfdom and slavery, around land tenure, around the relation of industrial combinations to workers, to each other and to the state, and around the position of minority groups in the pattern of state organization and activity.

The widening out of the world as a result of discovery of the hitherto unknown precipitated problems of expansion and interrelation of powers in a process of expansion which has puzzled statemakers for several centuries. Spanish, Dutch, French, German, Italian have alike been baffled by the difficulty of this area of adjustment.

Still more notably the shrinking of space, the widening of

[3] See Quincy Wright on *The Causes of War and the Conditions of Peace* (New York: Longmans, Green and Company, 1935), and his forthcoming study of this problem on a more elaborate scale.

education, the growth of horsepower and the mechanization of industry, combinations of labor and capital alike, have presented baffling control situations to the rulers of all lands. The ideologies of democracy, socialism, communism, fascism, nationalism, internationalism, religion, technocracy, racialism have shattered the peace of mind of state makers everywhere, and given them puzzles they could not solve.

It is possible and useful to consider some of the principal control points in our own day, without attempting any exhaustive listing of them and fully recognizing that they are in process of change.

One test of strategic points is made when a revolution occurs in a state. In this instance the question may be asked, What were the points seized by or controls inserted by the newly emerging group? Or the same thing may be seen in the gradual interpenetration of one state by another, as in the period of colonial expansion, most notably in the case of England—the most successful of the penetrating powers.

Revolutionists in our day will seize the organization of force, symbolic public buildings and properties, the organization of intercommunication and transportation, available gold, concentrations of food, fuel, and water supply. Thence they may reach out to forms of order and justice, to taxation and credits. With these established they may then advance to such controls as seem essential to the attainment of their social directives at the moment.[4]

The terroristic and spectacular reprisals of revolutionary moments have a dubious function, other than that of whip-

---

[4] Leon Trotzky, *History of the Russian Revolution.* Curzio Malaparte, *Coup d'Etat, the Technique of Revolution* (New York: E. P. Dutton and Company, Inc., 1932). Lyford Edwards, *Natural History of Revolution* (Chicago: The University of Chicago Press, 1927). L. P. Sorokin, *Sociology of Revolution* (Philadelphia: J. B. Lippincott Company, 1925). Article "Revolution" in *Encyclopedia of Social Sciences.*

ping up the spirits of the newly powerful and giving them
visible proof of their new estate, and the downfall and
humiliation of their foes. Further, the revolutionist's own insecurity is thereby made more secure. The old rulers whoever
they may be—the Czarists, the Kerenskyites, the Jews, the
liberals, the democrats, the bourgeois, the whites, reds,
blacks, or browns as the case may be provide the inflammable
material which the sparks of hate may kindle. Strategically
they may not be important, except in the important strategy
of symbolism.

The armed forces are the first prize, but it is not always
certain which way the guns will fire, if the morale of the army
and the police is dubious; the means of transportation and
intercommunication—symbols of science and change—are
perhaps next in order of consequence. Thus the control of the
radio alone in the Austrian uprising of 1934 proved almost
decisive in the false announcement of the abdication of the
ruler.

Gold will furnish the continuing means of support, without the use of force in its rawest forms, since gold is a form of
fluid power both within and without the state.

The symbolic maintenance of order and administration of
justice will exhibit the validity of the new claims to control.

And to the extent that there are dominant centers in the
land, it will be simpler to exert control from the possession of
a few of them, extending authority out from time to time.

Beyond this the discovery of the strategic points important and essential for the new program is far less simple.
Imprisonment, intimidation, execution, confiscation may
serve the purpose of the moment, but they are strong drinks
rather than steady diet; and must yield to more systematic
reorganization of power patterns in line with the new social

directives. Of course if the revolution is chiefly personal or factional the quantum of change will be very small, and perhaps in a little time imperceptible. Thus if one brother displaces the other, the alteration in control systems may be very slight.

But if there are deeper issues, the new group must then select the lines of reorganization to follow, and will then be confronted with the more complex problem of strategic selection of the lines of change. Thus in Russia the revolutionists reached for the land and the factories; in Germany for the destruction of the organized labor forces, the Jews, for a new land policy; in Italy for the reorganization of labor and industry, and against liberalism, masonry, socialism. In each instance the movement was accompanied by a bitter diabolizing of the enemy, by a dogmatic even if inconsistent ideology, and above all by a flaming type of symbolism burning with emotional appeal.

Like methods and results are observed in the invasion and conquest of other lands, in which the occupied territory must be reorganized. What shall be the official language of the newly conquered territory? What shall be the nature of the schools and the religion? If there are different types of law as in Czechoslovakia, where Russian, German, and Hungarian law mingles with the Roman, what shall emerge? Alsace-Lorraine, East Prussia, Ireland, and the Tyrol illustrate the difficulties in our own day of assimilation of new people under European conditions, dealing with similar racial types. *Commercium* and *connubium* have been sources of conflict from time immemorial.

The path of the conqueror is not as smooth as it seems even when the last center of armed resistance is broken down and when the country lies prostrate and broken. From that triumphant moment on, he may begin to learn of the poverty of power, and if wise will study the ways and means of attraction rather than those of enforced submission.

The steel framework of force will yield in importance to the patterns of progressive adaptation to strategic points in the cultural surroundings. That this is not impossible even under very adverse conditions is shown by the Romans and the British in the extension of their domains, but even in these states the difficulties of conciliation and assimilation are shown on many pages of tragic experience and bloody failure. Americans need not look beyond our own contacts with the Indians and the Negroes, on the one hand, or at the success of the "melting pot," on the other.

In revolution, insurrection, expansion of territory by conquest, purchase, or discovery, there may be seen many of the important strategic controls which are immanent in the political process. The types of resistance and the grooves of possible advance are sometimes more clearly revealed here than elsewhere in human experience, as in a lightning flash the darkness is driven back for an instant while the landscape of the scene is revealed.

But the strategy of control systems may also be observed in other situations than those just discussed, since broad sweeps of change are made by relatively peaceful processes. The smoothly running system of regulation requires the least force to supplement its own appeals and attractions. The success of the system is not measured by the number and variety of its controls, but by their strategic location in the given situation. The clumsier the system, the more obvious, disagreeable, and rough are its efforts at human conciliation and coöperation.

There is ample room for many "Essays in Persuasion" in

dealing with the strategic controls essential in any regime or any set of social directives. The bedside manner of the surgeon is important but that of the psychiatrist is more so. There is more psychiatry than surgery in planning. Many forms of control fall in the category of the chemical type or the glandular type—the formula of medication rather than of brute force.

The high purpose of statesmanship is the attainment of the recognized social objective with the greatest possible conservation of social energy, with the minimum of loss and the maximum of gain, taking the situation as a whole. From time to time the lines of regulation fall in different ways of life— affecting now one and now another set of values, interests, and symbols, and effecting a reorganization of them in more generally useful directions. Now it may be a religious area, now a territorial or neighborhood, now an industrial, now a cultural area. And always each area must be considered in relation to all the others, since the social pattern operates as a unit. That a relatively slight maladjustment in one zone may cause acute distress in many other zones is as true of the body politic as of the human organism.

In swiftly changing situations some values must be rudely disregarded, however respected otherwise. Thus in a fire the ordinary values are reversed, as axes, powerful streams of water, or dynamite are employed for the destruction of valuable property; household furnishings are roughly thrown out; women are snatched from their beds by men they have never met. Religious pictures may be cast out of the window; stocks, bonds, and currency are allowed to burn while a child or a dog is carefully rescued. In flood, famine, industrial panic, the value and behavior patterns are suspended or reoriented sometimes for the moment and sometimes forever, as new lines of organization and control emerge from obscurity.

The relatively simple case of traffic regulation illustrates the nature of strategic controls. In a possible system there might be no rules of the road whatsoever, or it might be required that every vehicle come to a full stop at every intersection, or that the speed limit should not exceed ten miles an hour; or that governors should be placed on all vehicles to ensure the rate of speed; or that some device be attached to motors indicating an excess rate of speed, and throwing out strips of paper with the rate of speed indicated, as once suggested to me by an enthusiast.

What happens is that strategic streets and intersections are chosen for stop lights or as one-way streets, that red glass reflectors are set up, that rates of speed are calculated at what is reasonable with changing motor development; that in consequence life and limb and property are safer, and that the tide of traffic is helped rather than hindered on the whole.

In building regulation, it would be possible to require a set form and type of construction, or indeed for the state to carry on the construction of all buildings. For the ordinary purposes of fire prevention, structural safety, and sanitation, however, the essential points in control are covered in a building code, leaving a wide range of option on the part of the builder. As time goes on it may be found wise to regulate the height of the building, or the type of building in a given district, or other characteristic features of construction may enter into the plan of control in the particular jurisdiction; and on to zoning. The political association may further begin the construction of certain types of structures, or even of all of them under some regimes.

In cultural fields such as religion and education, it has been found in many instances unnecessary to set up a monopoly of religion or of schools. State religion and no religion are the opposites, but between these extremes there is a wide gamut of other alternatives which may be utilized for the purposes of the community. Complete control of the schools or no public schools or support are the opposites in this field; and again there is a myriad of alternative solutions of this problem, varying widely in different systems.

In all of these cases the nature of the regulative system eases over gradually from the political to some other form, and social coöperation plays an important role in the process. Force alone does not function well in dealing either with the altar or with the classroom. It is not impossible to repress the value systems and interests centering around the church or the school, but the price is high and usually prohibitive.

The essence of organization is not roughness, as some seem to think, but management. Men may be influenced in many other ways than by pressure on the back or the buttocks with a strap. Behavior is successfully organized through medication, through diet, through training, through education. The human system may be reconditioned through the glands, perhaps; or the blood stream; or through any one of a thousand minor manipulations, stimulations, gradations, which move silently and subtly to their appointed end. There are psychiatrists who drive out the evil spirits; teachers who mold the mind without revolvers strapped to their side or spiked clubs in their hands. The strategy of control leans to the side of science rather than to the sword, to coöperation rather than coercion, to medicine, education, management rather than to violence or even to the sanctions of traditional law, to strategic minima rather than arrogant maxima.

In dealing with an intricate and sensitive industrial organization, strategic lines are even more significant, for

around them gather most thickly the clouds of misunderstanding and misinterpretation. Here the alternatives of state
monopoly and of laissez faire are most sharply presented and
most vigorously defended with warlike propagandas in full
swing. As already indicated, it is precisely in this field that
the antithesis between political controls and economic controls is most strongly emphasized. [5]

But exactly here the meaning of strategic controls is most
important and understanding most urgently required by the
higher statesmanship. Here the opportunity for penetrating insight and imaginative invention is richest. In a transition period such as ours, in which both government and
industry have been overwhelmed by technological change
upsetting the ancient landmarks, the necessity for reorganization is unparalleled in variety and reach. Here is an area in
which, if prejudices are overcome, it is possible to reach un-
realized capacities of advance, or in case of failure to precipitate the most violent periods of disorder, setting back social
development for many years or even generations.

The notion, however, that one, the political, is black and
the other, the economic, is white has acted as a barrier to
their legitimate union, or to a feeling that their progeny is of
illegitimate nature. It is with such a sentiment that fascism
has turned in the direction of the totalitarian state and communism in the direction of anarchism, with temporary gov-
ernmentalization of the industrial process as a whole. It is
this dogmatism that has stood in the way of breaking down
many of the barriers between types of direction which are
difficult to classify as economic or political, but which are
vitally necessary in the course of social development of
western nations.

[5] See chapter I.

It may be asked, What are some of these emerging and possible forms of adjustive action, on the border line between the classical political and the classical economic?[6] Some of these have already been considered but there are many others operating and others to be developed. Among these contrivances are such as the following examples of borderline activities:

Quasi-governmental corporations
Joint-stock participation by government and industry
Differential taxation
Contingent incorporation
Organization of coöperatives
Joint development of trade practices—codes
Licensing and regulation
Public works in relation to the business cycle
Semi-governmental control of money, banking, credit
Semi-governmental control of capital allocation, as in public utilities
Transportation and communication—services and rates
Land-tenure regulation and land use—mineral resources—water uses
Regulation of securities
Types of wage and price regulation
Validation or invalidation of contractual relations
Education
Health and recreation
Social security

Within this field there are innumerably varied types of strategic controls. In private enterprise controls have been

[6] J. M. Clark, *Social Control of Business* (Chicago: The University of Chicago Press, 1926). D. M. Keezer and Stacy May, *Public Control of Business* (New York: Harper and Brothers, 1930). B. E. Lippincott, *Government Control of the Economic Order* (Minneapolis: The University of Minnesota Press, 1935).

exercised by the possession of a relatively small but strategically important bottleneck in the enterprise. This is easily seen in railroading where the holding of a small line may be controlling; in mineral development where a small vein may prove decisive; likewise in the domain of water power where control may rise from a small stream or stretch; or a strip of land.

Industrial bottlenecks used for control and governmental controls are on a comparable level, in a study of regulation strategy.

Timber development may be determined by control of strategic locations essential to larger use. Military controls exercised through the holding of "commanding positions," have their analogies in civil relations.

Estimates of capacity for production and comments on the system of production may in themselves serve as useful forms of control, in the advisory and informative realm, without proceeding to direct indication of allocation within certain limits or otherwise. The possibilities in this direction have been considered in the case of public utilities subject to public regulation, and in dealing with exhaustible minerals. In time of stress, a War Industries Board went farther and established priorities of production.

Other types of controls may be established by what might be termed strategic rivalry. Just as private services may indicate to the government courses of action, so the state may indicate lines of activity which may lead to modifications of private behavior. The government may demonstrate a form of service, as in the case of a municipal electric lighting plant or a power plant, which may serve as an incentive or inducement to private owners to better their service or their rates.

Important forms of demonstrations are made by government, as for example, erosion demonstrations, housing developments, farm engineering; and the effect of these may be far-reaching. It is of course equally possible for private interests to demonstrate the usefulness of some form of public service which may subsequently be taken over by the political agency, as in the case of health demonstrations in many fields. In many communities there is wide opportunity for such reciprocal demonstration. New techniques are developed in this manner, often of the very greatest value to the civilization in which they are cultivated.

An important type of strategic control is exercised by means of rates for the transportation of persons and goods. Differential railway or other transportation rates may determine the fate of a community, and historically have been employed for that purpose. To the extent that such rates are controlled or directed by the government, it may exercise a pronounced influence on the location of industry and population. And this may be brought about without governmental ownership of transportation systems, if it is desired to do so.

In like manner extension of power service by electric lines and by differential rates is of far-reaching importance. Tariffs and subsidies are likewise powerful instruments in the determination of industrial policy, and constitute one of the most effective controls in the hands of political association. It has been suggested, for example, by an inventive mind that the government might effectively control the banking system by assuming the security function and delegating the others to banking institutions, perhaps first to wholesalers in money and credit and then by them on down to the local retailer in credit.

There are interests identified as "public" interests. In the United States business "affected with a public interest" is *pro tanto* declared to be subject to public regulation. But what constitutes a "public" interest as against a private interest; or when may a public interest rightfully impinge upon a private interest, or vice versa? These interests may be set forth in a declaration of public policy through the legislative body, but there is also the projection of the law through judicial interpretation, and to this development the jurist will direct his attention, searching for some principle which may illuminate the path of society.

From the point of view of this particular discussion, this search illustrates the shifting boundary lines between public and private relationships.

The law of contract also affords many examples of the zigzag boundary line between the public and the private.[7] What kinds of contracts are legally enforceable and under what conditions, with relation to the public interest especially? What is the nature of the agreement which can be enforced by the state, or will be? This problem arises in Moscow as readily as in Paris or London. There are, to be sure, contracts "contrary to public policy" which will not be protected at all; and a larger number on the border line between acceptability and indifference on the part of the state. We enforce some contracts within the borders of an industry but forbid types of contracts between industries if they promote monopoly. We forbid a wide variety of compacts inconsistent with the social policy of the time, selecting patterns of public approbation and disapproval.

When the human will is projected after death in the form of inheritance, other difficult problems of public policy arise, and many answers may be given as to the nature and condi-

---

[7] W. N. Hohfeld, "Fundamental Legal Conceptions as Applied in Judicial Reasoning," *Yale Law Journal*, XXIII, 1 (November 1913), pp. 16-59; XXVI, 8 (June 1917), pp. 710-770.

tions of inheritance in a given social order. The struggles over primogeniture and entail, over perpetuities, over death duties illustrate this further.

The question arises inevitably, What types of cases will be relegated to private determination, as by ecclesiastical courts, commercial courts, baseball judges, and what types held to be within the range of public review and protection? Precisely at this point it is possible to see clearly how the lines between public and private relationships shade over into each other.

It may be found useful to reconsider the concept of "ownership" and its various meanings in investment, management, control, influence upon human behavior.[8] The exclusive antithesis between private property and public property does not stand analysis, especially under modern conditions; and struggles based upon an assumption of complete exclusiveness assume an air of futilitarianism.

The problem of what may be called "privacy" and "publicity" is by no means peculiar to property relations, but runs through every way of social life. Is there to be found a sharp dividing line between what is private and what is public, and can that line once marked be held to be unchanging in its fixation, or will it be liable to alter under social pressure and notice?

A large part of the material property in any country is already public. Compute the streets, public ways and places in any city and it will appear that the city owns a large per cent of the total area of the town; compute the areas owned by the United States and the State and other subdivisions in the United States and it appears that a large per cent of the total is in the hands of the government.

[8] See J. R. Commons on *Legal Foundations of Capitalism* (New York: The Macmillan Company, 1924).

But more than that, in the complexity of modern industrial relations the problem of actual ownership becomes increasingly intricate. Is the particular industry owned by the majority of the stockholders, or by an active minority; or by the creditors; or by the managers whose skill is so indispensable that they can make or break the business; or perhaps by the bankers? Or perhaps the government may be a large owner in the banks that own the business that the shareholders or perhaps the bondholders think they own. When holding companies are superadded to this structure, the possibility of specifically allocating ownership, or of determining what is the significance of ownership becomes proportionally greater.

The relative roles and spheres of privacy and publicity are not as clearly defined as some may assume. What is private life and what is public life is not really fixed by a hard and fast line, which may be drawn once and for all, but is a flexible boundary.

A modern scientific world brings both greater publicity and greater privacy, paradoxically. Printing and reading, the radio, the phonograph, rapid transportation bring men together but they may also serve as the instruments of isolation. Privacy is more than a lodge in some vast wilderness. It may rest upon the deliberate cultivation of opportunities for the social organization of isolation. It is possible to reach a high point in the organization of social communication and participation and the values that arise from them, but it is equally possible, at the same time, to plan for the organization of areas of isolation and privacy—in the midst of an apparently congested civilization.

An individual in a public library may be isolated and enjoy privacy—the park service may organize the wilderness for him and keep it, or parts of it, isolated; he may tune in on or out of voices on the air—with modern communication he may retreat, far or near, as he wills; he may even lose himself in the crowd; or the group may organize the most remote retreat for him, as seen in the church and the hospital notably. The essence of the inner privacy and publicity is not determined by the scheme of political control, but by the value systems of the time, and the modes of their administration.

In conclusion, a nearer view of the control system shows a variety of interlacing systems, an intricate pattern of regulating and interregulating systems. Some of these are political, some are economic, some are familial, some are religious, some are cultural. Depending upon the type of social tension at a given time, one or the other of these regulative systems may be most active. Their functions are to some extent interchangeable—so that the cardinal once wore the ecclesiastical hat and the shirt of steel. New forms of regulative systems appear and disappear as the problems they confront burn into the picture and then fade out in the background. Pestilence, war, poverty, famine, fire and flood, invention, discovery, ideas, personalities shift the form of these patterns. In darker hours of crudeness, the hemlock, the cross, the firing squad are our guides; in happier moments conciliation, coöperation, consent, persuasion serve as the leaders of social change and devise the system to meet the newly emerging problem. Happy is the people with vision to discern early the signs of change, with swift intelligence to devise the modes of changing with change, with courage and faith to blend the old into the new before the evil spirits of pessimism and violence begin their dire work. The inventive faculty of man has not yet exhausted all the molds of ingenuity, all the models of coöperation, contrivance, association. History may be past politics, but politics must look forward as well as backward.

On the ingenuity and skill with which the social inventiveness of our time develops and the readiness with which inventive suggestions are received and made effective depend in large measure the future of our civilization. The old structures are always being outworn, but in a rapidly changing period such as ours, the tempo of change is very swift, and unless ingenuity, adaptation, and adjustment are equally fast, disaster is here.

The mold in which modern society and the modern state were cast is broken by modern science and technology. The new cathedral calls for the new master builders. The shuffling of many restless feet, the shrill voices of discontent arising in many lands—these are the sure signs of an impatience which cannot forever be satisfied with glorification of things as they are; of an impatience which experience teaches may ripen into actions of protest, violent and undiscriminating; of an impatience which may break a deadlock between politics and economics with the blows of force. The quantity of social control need not change, but its forms, types, lines are altered to meet new needs in new periods of tension.

In these critical moments it is important to look at the control and regulative systems as they actually are, not as we wish they were. True leaders will follow their problem where it leads, through the complicated labyrinths of human life through interests, ideas, values, following the way to effective forms of regulation which promote the happiness and security of mankind, no matter by what name they be called. Our guides need not look at the labels political, economic, social, but at the effects on human life and happiness. Long ago we were warned against putting new wine into old bottles. Out of the ferment of modern science, education, organization, technology, there will emerge new shapes and spirits of coöperation and control, with new institutions and values, facing a new civilization. For the life of life is changing its forms to fit its changing forces.

VI
THE NATURE OF NATIONAL
PLANNING

IN THE UNITED STATES more planning has been done than
elsewhere, both nationally, locally, and in the domain of
industrial enterprise, contrary to the common conclusion.
The Constitution itself was the most important piece of planning in its time. The only comparable efforts were the French
constitutions of the Revolutionary period, which proved incapable of reconciling the diverse interests of that stormy
period. The prevailing doctrine of that day, which it was the
rankest heresy to dispute, was that constitutions and governments could not be made by the voluntary act of man, but
must either be set up by divine power or develop as a slow
growth. In Paris, London, and Berlin the formation of a constitution was as impossible as it was impious. The deliberate
organization of a new government, in which hereditary political rule was abolished, in which responsible and representative government was set up, in which the outlines of political
action were traced, including even the mode of change of the
government—all this was anathema to those who devoutly
believed that governments could not be planned but must be
framed outside of human will. They denounced all such planning in set terms, "political planning" they called it in pro-
foundest scorn.

Nor was the Constitution a purely political document. It
was devised to meet a crisis both in industry and in government
which threatened the stability of both. The new instrument

of government contained important provisions regarding taxation, tariffs, commerce—in short it was a plan for economico-political operation on a grand scale. It was the most monumental heresy of the eighteenth century and denounced by all but the revolutionaries of that day. The plan of the Constitution was followed by the abolition of the old land system providing for primogeniture and entail, which with the hereditary transmission of political power was the bulwark of the autocratic system of that day. Hamilton's plan for manufactures was the next heroic piece of American planning. This was followed by Gallatin's efforts and by the Great Plan of John Adams for the federal lands. Clay planned the "American system," as it was called, of tariff. The homestead act of 1862 provided for a system of land acquisitions which gave a tract of land to almost any applicant, and laid the basis for our whole scheme of land tenure in the West. The national banking system was planned and unplanned as a part of our national policy.

Down to the Civil War, no nation had done more deliberate national planning in experimental fields, both economic and political, than the United States, with the exception of France whose plans had not turned out so fortunately.

Following the Civil War came the rapid rise of the large-scale industries, and the era of large-scale industrial planning. The Taylor-Emerson-Gant systems came into vogue; efficiency and management were studied and developed; large-scale machinery and plants were constructed; production, financing, salesmanship were extended over what in earlier times would have seemed fantastic areas. America became the home of quantity production and widespread long-time plans for development of various industries, imitated to some extent by other nations, and in particular by Russia when it came to industrialize its people and called upon American engineers and industrialists to execute the task.

The weakness of business planning alone is soon revealed in a period of active operation. The difficulties may be summarized as follows:

1. Business can secure effective coöperation only within the limits of an independent business enterprise. Different undertakings have no common authority to maintain a common program of action, and hence efforts in that direction are likely to prove negative and wasteful rather than positively productive either of advantage socially or profit personally.[1]

2. Business planning aims at profit which may or may not be socially advantageous in a given instance, and may readily lead to wide discrepancies in the distribution of income, with repercussions again on consumption.

3. Business cannot protect itself against the recurring hazards of the business cycle, and hence is forced to appeal to government itself from time to time for protection against evils it cannot control. The combination movement in industry is an effort to eliminate some of the hazards from which business cannot save itself. "Business planning has found no way to prevent the growth of factors that tend to make the business cycle more hazardous. Indeed the hazard grows greater in large part because of business planning itself."

4. Furthermore the planning of great corporations and the systems in vogue among agricultural producers do not synchronize or harmonize, and in consequence there may be disastrous gaps between the economic situation of one and the other.

Consequently it follows that when the government at-

[1] Taken largely from the *Final Report* of the National Planning Board (1933-1934), Federal Emergency Administration of Public Works (Washington, D. C.: Superintendent of Documents, 1934), p. 21.

tempts planning in these fields it is attacking problems of enormous difficulty which no one has yet solved. It is not making inexpert attempts to do what business itself accomplishes satisfactorily. "So far as government succeeded in finding solutions it would be broadening and making safer the field of private enterprise."

The city planning movement in the United States began later than in many European cities but made rapid headway once it was launched at the beginning of the nineteenth century.[2] There are now some nine hundred city planning boards in the United States, with some 250 county planning boards, some forty-six State planning boards, and regional agencies, such as the Pacific Northwest, New England, and the TVA.

Various misapprehensions regarding the nature and tendencies of planning have misled many persons. Among these is the idea that all planning is centralized national planning developed at and emanating from some fixed point of authority. In some tension situations and on some political and social levels of habitation this might be the case; but in democratic societies strategic planning is an enterprise in which many different levels of activity are involved.

There will be national planning and various types of local planning. There will be planning suggestions from public, private, and semi-public agencies of all sorts. Unquestionably there must be a central directive and a unified general system of regulatives, but there are metes and bounds within this larger framework; there are circles of influence and activity within the greater circle; and all of these agencies may react upon each other without preventing the general concert of action which is to be attained.

[2] Thomas Adams, *Outline of Town and City Planning* (New York: Russell Sage Foundation, 1935).

Planning does not involve a fixed and unchangeable system which might be clamped down like a steel frame on soft flesh. Planning is a continuous process involving continuous readjustment and revision to meet changing situations as they arise. "The national life is like a moving wave in which a new equilibrium must constantly be found as it sweeps forward." This is true even of physical planning and even more applicable in the case of more delicate forms of planning.

It is false and misleading to assert that all planning involves regimentation, using this term to mean arbitrary and autocratic action, the equivalent of oppression. First of all, liberty exists only in some ordered framework of operations and understandings. Without these understandings as to the protection of liberty and without their implementation there could be no domain of non-interference. In the operations of government this is fairly well understood, but not yet fully recognized in the areas called the economic, where the idea of laissez faire still survives, long after it has been replaced by a more constructive idea in the political world. The truth is that the inner areas of spontaneity and creative impulse need to be protected by the general regulative system in order that they may attain their most complete development. In a very real sense we may and do plan for liberty of action as well as for restraint of action. Paradoxical as it may seem to some the governmental system may cultivate individual initiative growth and development, instead of repressing and crushing it down and out.

It may readily be conceded that this has not always been the guiding star of all governments in all times and places, but there are brilliant illustrations of the possibilities in this direction; and in a period of more intelligent social direction the range of possibility is greater than ever.

Wise planning deals with the "zoning of power," with the broad diffusion of initiative and responsibility most conducive to the welfare of the group at a given stage of its development. It is quite possible for the state to be legally, in the narrower sense of the term, omnipotent and irresistible, while in actual practice very wide areas of behavior are left wide open for local and individual initiative. This indeed is as true of industrial organization as it is of political or ecclesiastical for that matter. There is as much initiative in the French nation today as there ever was in the French feudality of centuries ago. There was as much liberty in the United States after the Constitution was adopted as there was in Rhode Island before that event. There is no guarantee that, say, three men working for an employer on a small scale will be any more free than three thousand working for a larger concern.

The strategy of planning involves then the kind of prevision that contemplates zones or areas of independent initiative, territorially, individually, and associationally, if there were such a word. Congestion and overcentralization are among the very gravest diseases of the body politic, and judgment and foresight are indispensable if they are to be averted. But this is not a pot that can be left to boil without attention; it must be carefully watched by experienced persons. The strength and direction of social change is the key to the type of organization feasible at a given phase of development in a society.

It is commonly taken for granted that liberty is protected chiefly by the courts. The judicial agencies play their part in this process, but in large measure the administrative agencies supply the "zoning of power" upon which the growth and play of individual initiative rely for their protection and stimulation. The degree of initiative within the administration itself, the readiness with which it accepts suggestions from outside, the facility with which it is able to effect friendly and coöperative relations with various non-governmental or quasi-governmental associations of variegated types; these are factors that will be effective in determining the scope of free play of activities outside the formal framework of regulation. Legal omnipotence is not inconsistent with administrative amiability and administrative fostering of initiative.

The test of planning is not whether it may for the moment set up a new series of regulations, inevitable in a period of readjustment, but whether the new pattern taken as a whole opens the way for a wider range of human activity and happiness. The temporary outline of a form of order may be the task of the policeman, but the larger and more enduring pattern will be worked out with the aid of the planner.

In this task science, education, skillful administration, organized persuasion are far more effective than the sword or the gun. The swashbucklers are seldom the statesmen. And the warriors who really fight, as distinguished from those who know how to make gestures and declaim, are seldom social planners, although there have been some notable exceptions to this broad statement. Their very elaborate planning is designed for war.

An unwarranted assumption in the discussion of regimentation is that in the absence of governmental regulation there is no equivalent regulation by some one else. This is falsified by human experience, which shows that arbitrary and oppressive control of individuals has arisen again and again—is indeed the commonplace of human relations. To ignore this is to pass by our basic experience in government. To break down petty forms of oppression exercised by one man over another has been historically one of the very great tasks of the political association. The emancipators may have utilized this power for their own selfish purposes, but they were able to function because the balance was in their favor—they gave more than they took. The order and justice of the national state was better than that of the feudal organization. The great lords were better received than the petty lordlets of the locality. The King's highway, the King's justice came to be accepted as deliverance rather than oppression, in the first stages of the larger area or unit of authority.

Again and again the state has intervened to protect the weak against the strong, to restrict the regimentation of tenants by their landlords, of servants by their masters, of employees by their employers. To assume that no group except the government has the urge or tendency to oppress individuals is to ignore the most obvious facts of human experience—to refuse to look at the monumental evidence showing the cruelty of man to man on every level of action.

While many of the oppressions of the old land system have been eliminated from modern practice, many remain, and while the private regimentation seen in human slavery has been abolished, there remain wide areas of private regimentation in the swiftly changing industrial order. Here the tempo has been so fast that the usual trade customs and ethics have been left behind in many cases, and the new rulers have been almost unrestricted in the exercise of vast powers over the lives and fortunes of workers. Employment, wages, working conditions, insurance were in private hands without the earlier responsibility for the serf or slave. Price fixing, production control, credits, and a long series of far-ranging powers were placed in the hands of individuals or small groups without any practical restraint upon them, and with the inevitable appearance of widespread oppression—not by government—but in such cases by private groups or persons.

In many ways of life, the choice is not between regimentation and no regimentation, but between public control and private regimentation, between two systems of regulation, one in responsible and the other in irresponsible hands. The more rapid the course of change, the greater the likelihood that new controls will be set up in one way or another. The reconstruction of these regulative systems in terms of social control rather than the old-time political or the so-called purely economic is one of the greatest tasks of the modern planner of social organization. The values and ideologies underlying the old system are not readjusted to emerging values and systems rapidly enough to avoid misunderstanding and friction, and herein lies the largest possibility of unbalance in the social and political order. The maintenance of the moving equilibrium at this point is consequently one of the major tasks of strategic planning in our day.

This, moreover, is not merely a task of democratic statesmanship, but equally of Fascist, Nazi, Communist, Japanese statesmanship and of any and all other states in which technological and other changes are proceeding rapidly and demanding urgently the reorganization of institutions and the reorientation of our ideas and value systems at many important points.[3]

Some basic assumptions underlie modern planning, whether explicitly recognized or not.

[3] On value systems, see *Recent Social Trends*, p. lxxv. See analysis of modern planning systems in the *Final Report* of the National Planning Board, 1934. See also Wesley C. Mitchell, *Business Cycles, the Problem and Its Setting* (New York: National Bureau of Economic Research, Inc., 1927), p. 172.

1. One of these is the recognition of the importance of an over-all framework of social control of the general type known as the state.

2. The reorganization of the regulative system in terms of social-political planning and adjustment.

3. The recognition of areas of self-activity into which the state will not ordinarily penetrate, and which it will strive to foster and protect.

4. The reorganization of the regulative system in terms of modern science, technology, education.

5. The recognition and protection of value systems other than political within the framework of the political association.

6. The importance of coördinating national and local policies, public, quasi-public, and private plans, instead of allowing them to drift apart or pull against each other.

These assumptions apply to modern industrial states generally, regardless of the differences in organization and ideology and are indeed accepted in part by all of them, but not as a whole.[4]

1. That there shall be a general framework of regulation of the general form of the modern state is generally recognized, but with this there goes many times the assumption that there is a "natural" economic order and a "natural" system of economic controls which the state should in the main accept. Since the general abandonment of the classical laissez-faire system, this doctrine is no longer as clearly stated, but it persists as a basis of resistance to the development of types of social control cutting through the older lines of classification.

2. This negative position appears more clearly when the reorganization of the regulative system in terms of social-

[4] On the Japanese planning system see H. Moulton's *Japan* (Washington, D.C.: The Brookings Institution, 1931). R. Fujisawah, *Recent Aims and Political Development of Japan* (New Haven: Yale University Press, 1923).

political adjustments enters into the discussion openly. Here the tacit assumption just discussed becomes explicit and even strident in emphasis and tone.

The outworn philosophy of Smith and Marx, interpreted by Spencer, is reinstated and reëstablished, and the dogma expressly asserted that there is a well-defined economic domain, an exclusive and self-regulative domain into which government should not enter, or only under exceptional circumstances. Less government in business may become the slogan, or less regulation of industry, or criticism of governmental action as socialistic or communistic, always with the assumption that there really is a self-regulating system of economics which *if left alone* will automatically produce the greatest flow of utilities for the society.

The whole course of western social legislation for the last hundred years is against this assumption or conclusion, as we survey the successive waves of governmental regulation of the abuses of private control of mines, factories, housing, investment, insurance, down the long sweep of the modern shore, and the growth of monopoly in industry itself. Industry has over and again invoked the aid of government to save itself from unfair competition. In the face of increasing concentration of financial control, in the face of swiftly changing technology with its effects upon economic and political institutions, in the face of the widespread unrest in all classes of society, this doctrine is rapidly crumbling. But precisely here we observe that the very insecurity of the doctrine has been the incentive to the most frantic efforts to maintain and protect it—even to the breaking of the established molds of order, justice, and liberty in such states as Germany and Italy.

3. A part of the fury of this defense of an outlived dogma

is the failure to reckon with the third assumption of modern planning; namely, the necessity of recognizing areas of self-activity into which the state will not ordinarily penetrate, but which it will constructively labor to foster and protect. This is not a doctrine exclusively applicable to economic zones of behavior, but a more general social principle running through the whole gamut of government and social functions. At times this policy has not been the result of the moderation of the governors who were bent on taking everything there was, but of the operation of what I have elsewhere called the poverty of power.

In later times formal defenses were built up against the oppressive behavior of autocratic rulers, and in still more recent times there sprang up the recognition of the immense value of self-activity, of initiative, of spontaneity of spirit, and of the priceless value of fostering the growth of these traits and skills in any community struggling for higher standards of life.

To this doctrine and its elaboration many of the old-time economists contributed, notably Mill. But, by the peculiar twist they gave to the idea, they often made it serve the purpose of blocking measures of social control adapted to that very purpose. Thus public education was opposed by Mill and Spencer on the ground of its interference with private liberty—while the individual was by the same logic kept ignorant of his own possibilities and enslaved by his lack of learning.

In the broader sense the principle is essentially sound, however, and constitutes one of the basic elements in national planning. In high-tension moments and in particular directions this area may be restricted and narrowed, but in the long trend, the zoning of power will lead to the release of

the creative faculties of mankind, and will positively constitute this as one of the social directives of the state. It is not
unlikely that impatience may discover an unusual and unnecessary number of fictitious emergencies as a cloak for
arbitrary power, but the higher strategy will leave the way
clear for the largest possible areas of initiative.

4. Another basic assumption is that the regulative system
must be reorganized in terms of modern science, technology,
and education. This presupposes a set of general attitudes
based upon the acceptance of these elements as essential to
the orderly conduct of life in modern societies. It presupposes
peoples who are, so to speak, science-minded, technology-
minded, education-minded, facing the implications of modern science and technology and realizing the possibilities of
modern educational process. Many western peoples are familiar with the trends of science in the broadest sense and
with some of the mechanical developments resulting from it,
skilled in the manipulation of the new mechanical controls, or
chemical and biological controls, or through agriculture and
otherwise. But the relationship of these revolutionary controls to social processes or to governmental processes is often
either incomplete or indeed almost entirely missing. Many
accept the results of science in gadget form, but do not enter
into its methods and its spirit—the use of a perfected invention, but not its social implications. The machine master
looking forward eagerly to every new and latest development
in his special field may live in a governmental world of a century ago; and not only this but he finds a moral purpose and
necessity in so doing. He is as proud of tradition in the one
case as he is eager to abandon it in the other. He is as ashamed
to be old-fashioned in the one case as he is anxious to be
labeled old-fashioned in the other; and he does not see the in-

congruity in his attitudes. He may cling to an outworn local government, such as a township, as enthusiastically as he hastens on the other hand to find the latest model of an automobile. He may be in antagonism to planning in public affairs as much as he favors it in private affairs; and more surprising still he may oppose planning on the ground that science makes it impossible; that we cannot plan because of the rapidity of change which might outmode the plans in the future. Thus it appears that we must not plan because we cannot change our ancient traditions; and on the other hand because there is too much change. With even greater folly it may be asserted that the educational system with all of its scientific equipment and its trained personnel must be devoted to the perpetuation of outmoded doctrines, and even that competing doctrines must not be a subject of discussion. Thus creative ability would be employed to produce sterility, and science to train for non-science.

The assumption of the modern state builder who wishes to advance other than by means of violence and brutal regimentation must be that the emerging regulative system will recognize the pattern of scientific and technological change in an educational setting as the basis of continuing reorganization. Without this western civilization is doomed.

5. Another fundamental assumption is that of the necessity of the recognition and protection of value systems other than political within the political association. This is often the *pons asinorum* of the *Politiker*. They are by temperament, training, experience concerned with political values, and, further, their prestige is dependent upon the inflation of the political in the social system. The governors are accordingly inclined to look upon government as the most important thing in the community, and to underrate the meaning of other

forms of social interest and concern or even look upon them as competitors to be closely watched and shrewdly checked.

The doctrine of the sovereign state is intoxicating to the light-headed, who conclude that because they may lawfully do anything, practically they may do all things. The modern totalitarian state is the inebriated state of sovereignty in which unsteady rulers roughly attempt to assimilate every other form of association to that of the state—labor unions, cultural associations, industry, and even the church. If such a result were actually attained, what would happen within the shell of the new totalitarianism would be the rise of value systems under other names but performing like functions. Men might salute the state or even wear its uniform, but the soul would be another soul and the spirit another spirit. The state itself would find it convenient to encourage independent centers of spontaneity even on its own. The reconciliation of other value systems and their coördination in a growing concern may be and usually is one of the most perplexing problems of statesmanship, but it may also be said that for this hour came they into the kingdom. Rulers would not be rulers in an automatic society, or if termites are cited per contra, it may be said they would not worry about their problems.

The old tendency was for the state to ride roughshod over other elements, misjudging its own relative significance and the priority of its own projects. For this reason, it is important that it be set up as a basic assumption of the state planners that they shall constantly bear in mind the importance of recognition and protection of other values than their own. This constant reminder may serve as a guide in the conduct of state affairs, as a warning against overexaggeration of state claims and failure to face the realities of associated life in a social group.

It must be recognized that there are human situations in which the reconciliation of these competing values is impossible on anything but a low level of concurrence in which violence will probably play a large and bloody role. History is unfortunately full of pictures where such methods were employed whether wisely or unwisely in a special case, as England and Ireland, Germany and the Poles, Austria-Hungary and its five nationalities. But history is also full of brilliant illustrations of statesmanship such as that of modern Switzerland which reconciled in incredible fashion diverse and conflicting interests and brought them to a relatively high level of concurrence, partly by arms perhaps but in considerable measure by the arts of persuasion and management. The British Empire and the United States are modern examples of the strategy of interest reconciliation—not, to be sure, without a darker side in each of these cases, but yet with a conspicuous preponderance of deliberate design to conciliate. These are cases where the negativism of fear was more than offset by the positivism of symbolic attraction to the shelter of a protecting association hospitable to free development of variety. Pantheons in religion, parliaments in politics, equality before the law, even-handed justice, equality in conditions of exchange—these are symbols of conciliation that have played important parts in the cohesion of great states. It is policies of this type that may safely be assumed as basic in a large scheme of national planning.

Value systems it may be said can be crushed out by fire, by sword, by persistent cruelty and unrelenting persecution, as religions and races have been crushed down and out. But the price paid is high and even then the result may not follow. Was the wrath of Spain against the Jew or of Germany against the non-Aryans of our own time socially valuable? Or of the French against the Huguenots, or of the Austrians against the Hussites in Bohemia? A surgical operation with a battle axe may be inferior to medication, diet, relaxation, and the modern series of roads back to normalcy.

6. A final assumption of planning is that various types of plans must be considered in relation to each other, and their programs and implications taken under advisement. Central and local plans of government, plans of quasi-public agencies, plans of private industry, plans of voluntary associations of a great variety; all of these must be related to each other. It is not essential that the government shall dictate all of these plans but that it should know what is doing, what the tendencies and implications of various designs may be, in order that the central planners may govern themselves accordingly. It must know the general patterns of plans in order to frame an intelligent plan of its own—not to dictate or even modify all other plans but to serve as the basis for an over-all type of planning. Each motorist, in order to steer his own course, must know what the courses of others are likely to be, as to speed, direction, modifiability, and so on. So the state must know what it may reckon upon in speed, direction, and concurrence or collision in relation to other associational groupings within its jurisdiction. Thus a public-works program, or a public educational program, or a credit program is related to other like programs and must be considered in this light.

In high-tension moments in the life of the group as a whole as in war or other life and death situations, such as fire, flood, famine, plague, the state will be likely to give its own plans sweeping priority. But in other phases of state development, the lines will be far looser and the intent and extent of state interest far less conspicuous and its modes of effecting the priority of its conclusions far less abrupt.

In the wider circle of international relations it is likewise essential that plans be considered in relation to each other. This is true even in the absence of an established jural world order, in which the elements of justice are consistently administered. Indeed the failure of such an order makes it all the more necessary that each member of the family of nations be familiar with the high strategy of the planners of other states, and consider their bearings on their own plans. And again this is equally true whether intentions are friendly or hostile. On a friendly basis there are modifications and interrelations that may be suggested; and on a hostile basis the plans of other states are essential for an understanding of the nature of the enemy power.

Under modern conditions other groups than the state often make their plans across state lines, as science, religion, labor, and high finance, and will unquestionably continue to do so whatever national walls may be built for political purposes. At this point the political association lags behind other important forms of associated life; and the lag if prolonged will precipitate serious consequences for social adjustment— has already done so on a colossal scale. In any case, and whatever the theory or program of international relations, the national planner cannot neglect the affairs and the plans of other states. At every step, as in the use of minerals, water power, food supplies, markets, security—all these on the simplest level—the international aspect of national planning becomes evident. Intercommunication will make this increasingly apparent and isolation correspondingly difficult. The radio and the aeroplane are products of science with wide-ranging influence on the form and method of political association; and they are only the advance guard of technology.

CONCLUSION

If the foregoing propositions are accepted as true, it is of great importance to search diligently for the strategic directive devices in any given society or phase of it, in order that the regulative system may be set up and operated with the least friction and wastage of effort. The formalism of the law, however, the mechanistic nature of much governmental theory and practice, and the neutral attitude of many classical or neo-classical economists make this by no means an easy task in our time. The will to search, the spirit of imagination, inventiveness, and social insight are essential, to say nothing of the popular attitudes upon which any such program may rest in the last analysis.

There have been, however, and still are constructive jurists, inventive statesmen, and contriving economists who are available for this high enterprise—students and practitioners of social technologies whose faculties are equal to the occasion. Some of these workers may be engineers, some may be teachers, research men, and scientists of all types—some may be doctors, some may be psychologists, psychiatrists, psychoanalysts, psychosynthesists, or whatever color they fly in this division. Others may be statesmen, priests, industrialists, leaders of labor, workers with men. Some will be leaders acclaimed by thousands; others obscure workers. The overwhelming danger is, as few statesmen have recognized, that they will not be able to keep pace with the tempo of modern invention, and the barbarians will take the tools of science for their own purposes. [5] The slow-moving battalions of science will arrive one day, and the reorientation of under-

---

[5] To this H. G. Wells is a brilliant exception. See his work *The Shape of Things to Come*; also *The World of William Clissold, Work and Welfare.*

standings and value systems based on earlier systems of intelligence now outgrown will also come; but it may be too late.

In the preceding pages I have indicated some of the important lines of control, and I have suggested some other types; but this is only a beginning of a long and difficult task of peering into the nature of social relationships, and of molding out of new insights the significant tools of new organization.

It will be essential in this undertaking to dissipate the fogs of Smith-Spencer and Marx-Lenin; to reorient the widespread misunderstanding regarding the real role of traditions in group life; to break through the entrenched opposition of those to whom change is an interference with their status and with the value system in which their prestige is set firmly. But the alternative to constructive social initiative, to integration and reorganization, in terms of modern life and its direction and tempo, is not pleasant to contemplate by those who do not regard violence as the *summum bonum* of existence.

All this is not the work of an hour or a day. Nor is this the task for those with faint hearts or soft heads, for those who "wish well feebly," or those who enjoy a flabby and selfish happiness in a troubled world. It will call for hearts as stout and hands as strong as those of the American pioneers, skills of machinery and management of the best American models, leadership and ideals of the highest American type.

For my part I do not believe that America stands at the broken end of a worn-out way. Vistas of wider prosperity than ever stretch out before us; higher standards of American living; finer achievements in American liberty, equality, and justice, if we have the wit, the will, the faith, the courage to reach out and take them—to utilize the heritage of American natural and human resources—the richest gift to any modern state.[6]

---

[6] In another study to be published shortly I consider the competing systems of superiority and solidarity, their philosophies, implications, and programs.

INDEX

INDEX

ADMINISTRATION, 128-129
Anarchism, philosophy of, 14-15, 27, 33, 89
   influence on Marx, 16-17, 23, 26, 113
   social democrats and, 31
Austin, John, 29-34

BERGSON, *Two Sources of Morality and Religion*, 41
Bodin, 30-32, 61

CHANGE, social, conservation and, 79-102
   invention and, 55-57, 81, 91-100, 104-105, 113, 120-122, 131, 136, 141-142
   pessimism and, 71-77
   politics and, 13, 30, 36-37, 55-59, 61-65, 79-102
   strategic controls and, 103-112, 120-122
   violence and, 29, 66-71, 106-109
Church, social control and, 38-41, 43, 46-47, 54-55, 58-59
   modifiability of, 82
   strategic controls and, 111-112, 120
   totalitarian state and, 137
Class, 21-22, 29, 62, 68, 86
Classical economists, 15-16, 23-28, 34, 79
Collectivism, 14-15, 23, 32-34
Conciliation, 90-91, 97, 100, 109, 120, 138
Conservation, 79-102, 110
Conservatism, 87-90
Constitutions, 62-63, 65, 123-124
Contract, law of, 117
   social, 35, 73
Control systems
   social control—political, economic, religious, cultural, familial, 14-15, 25-28, 34, 35-59, 80, 82, 90, 103-122, 131-135
   strategic controls, 103-122

Coöperation, 23, 39, 85, 109, 112, 120, 122, 125
Corporations, 41, 47-54, 114, 125

DARWINIAN theory, 55, 72-73, 79-81, 96
Decentralization, 37, 51
Defeatism, 71-72
Democrats, social, 29, 31
Democracy, 31, 55, 57, 64, 71, 80-81, 106-107, 126, 131
Determinism, 20, 23, 29, 73-77, 80-81
Divine right, 35, 38

ECONOMICS, borderline relations between politics and, 42-54, 56, 114-120
   boycott of government and, 14-29, 33-34, 58
   change and, 91, 94-95
   control system, as a, 35-59, 112-122, 131-133
   lack of balance between politics and, 13, 33-34, 56-57, 59, 113, 131
   laissez faire (*see* Laissez faire)
   Marxian (*see* Marx)
   planning and, 124-128, 131-133
Education, 47, 48, 58, 66, 86, 90-95, 97, 111-112, 114, 129, 132, 134-136
Evolution, biological, 72, 79-81, 92, 101
   economic, 19-20, 43, 70, 79
   political, 79-102
Executive, 35, 37, 49

FAMILY, 38-39, 41, 43, 54, 58, 82, 105, 120
Fascism, 67, 106, 108, 113, 131
Filmer, Sir Robert, *Patriarcha*, 38
Force, 15, 22, 68, 69, 71, 100, 106-110, 112, 121
Freud, 35, 75-76

GOVERNMENT, boycott of, 13-34, 58-59
change and, 61-66, 69, 79-102
glorification of, 29-34, 58
planning and, 123-143
social control and, 27-28, 35-39, 103-122

HARTMANN, *Philosophy of the Unconscious*, 72-74
Hegel, 18, 20, 24, 29-31, 33-34, 72-74, 75-76, 80
Hitler, 40, 43, 70, 71, 86
Hoover, *Challenge to Liberty*, 27
Huxley, 77, 79, 99

INDIVIDUALISM, 15-16, 23
Industry, borderline relations between politics and, 42, 52-54, 56, 114-119
change and, 63-64, 79, 87, 92, 95, 99
planning and, 123-143
social control and, 27-28, 38, 41-42, 47-59
strategic controls and, 109-110, 112-119
Intelligence, 62, 72-77, 92, 98, 101, 120
Invention, planning and, 135-136, 141
social change and, 90, 92, 94-95, 96-98, 100
social control and, 41, 55, 104-105, 113, 120-121, 141

KROPOTKIN, 14

LABOR, 23, 88, 106, 108, 140
Laissez faire, change and, 79-80, 95
classical economists and, 14-16, 21, 23-28, 31, 33-34
planning and, 127, 132-133
social control and, 48, 113
Legislation, 31, 62, 63-64, 90, 91, 95-96, 133
Lenin, 17, 67-68, 142
Liberty, 30, 46, 80, 127, 128, 133, 134, 142

MARX, boycott of government and, 14-29, 31, 34, 38, 88-89, 133, 142
change and violence and, 62, 66, 68, 72

Materialism, 20, 72-73
Meinecke, *Staatsräson*, 32
Militarism, 32, 33, 70-71
Mill, John Stuart, 20, 23-25, 34, 38, 134
Mitchell, Wesley C., 44-45
Modifiability, limits of, 82-87
Mumford, *Technics and Civilization*, 104
Mussolini, 40, 70-71
Mutation, 65-66, 79, 81-90, 100
Mutual aid, 14

NATIONALISM, 32-33, 48, 106
Natural law, philosophy of, 24-27, 132-133
Nazis, 67, 74, 131
Nietzsche, 67-69

OWNERSHIP, concept of, 118-119

PARTIES, 35, 90
Persuasion, 41, 86, 90, 91, 95, 120
Pessimism, 61, 71-75, 120
Planning, basic assumptions underlying, 131-143
business and industrial, 124-126
city, 126
nature of, 126-131
political, 63, 123-124
Plato, 61
Politics, borderline relations between economics and, 42-54, 56, 114-120
change and, 61-65, 79-102
lack of balance between economics and, 13, 33-34, 56-57
planning and, 35-39, 123-143
social control and, 35-59, 103-122
theories distorting role of, 13-34
Power, political, 16-17, 39, 41, 46, 77, 84, 103, 107, 109, 134
Pressure groups, 35
Privacy and publicity, 118-120
Production, change and, 91-92, 124, 130-131
Marx and, 18-19, 21-22, 24, 26, 31
social control and, 46, 50, 57-58, 115
Proletariat, 17, 21, 26, 70, 89
Propaganda, 18, 20, 22, 23, 28, 77, 90
Property, 110-111

Proudhon, 14
Psychiatry, 75-76, 110, 112, 141
Psychology, 35, 47, 59, 141
"Public" and "private" interests, shifting boundary lines between, 116-118

Radicalism, 87-89
Regimentation, 51, 127-131
Religion, evolution and, 81-82
    planning and, 138, 140
    social control as a, 22, 35, 39-40, 46-47, 57, 108, 110, 112, 120
Revolution, 24, 68, 70, 81, 93, 104, 106-109
Ricardo, 23-24, 26, 28

Schopenhauer, *World as Will*, 72-74
Science, change and, 73, 81, 89-95, 98, 101
    planning and, 132, 135-136, 140
    social control and, 58-59, 107, 112, 121-122
Smith, Adam, 20, 25, 133, 142
Socialism, 20, 28, 30, 33, 71, 80, 106, 108, 133
Socialization, 31, 32, 33, 56, 59, 99
Sorel, 67-71, 96
Sovereignty, doctrine of state, 30, 32, 81, 137

Spencer, Herbert, 27, 63, 72, 79-80, 133-134, 142
Spengler, *The Decline of the West*, 74
State, boycott of, 13-29, 33-34, 58-59
    change, methods of, and, 61-102
    glorification of, 14, 29-34, 58
    legal omnipotence of, 30, 84, 128-129
    planning, 123-143
    social control and, 35-59, 103-122
    sovereignty, 30, 32, 81, 137
Survival of the fittest, 55, 72-73, 79-81
Symbolisms, 40, 41, 47, 86, 100, 107, 108

Taxation, 39, 48, 51, 65, 106, 114
Technology, 28, 45, 57, 59, 81, 88, 91-93, 96, 113, 121-122, 131-133, 135-136, 140-141
Tolstoi, 14
Totalitarian state, 31-34, 113, 137
Tradition, 36, 92, 98, 100, 135-136, 142

Utilitarians, 35

Violence, 13-15, 66-71, 96-101, 106-109

War, 51-52, 68-71, 90-91, 99-100